CHRYSANTHEMUMS

Batsford Books on Horticulture
Advisory Editor: C. D. Brickell
Director, Royal Horticultural Society's Garden, Wisley

James F. Smith

CHRYSANTHEMUMS

B.T. Batsford Ltd
London & Sydney

Published in association with
The Royal Horticultural Society

First published 1975
© James F. Smith 1975

ISBN 0 7134 2936 4

Printed in Great Britain by
Cox & Wyman Ltd
London, Fakenham and Reading
for the publishers B. T. Batsford Ltd
4 Fitzhardinge Street, London W1H 0AH
and 23 Cross Street, Brookvale, NSW, 2001 Australia

Contents

List of Illustrations

Illustrations 1–9 are between pages 40 and 41; 10–20 between pages 104–105.

Colour Plates

Line Drawings

Acknowledgements

During the many years I have been associated with growing this wonderful flower, many sincere and long-lasting friendships have been made. This has been demonstrated in no uncertain manner by the help and guidance freely given me when I embarked upon writing this book. It is true that many books about chrysanthemum culture have been written over the years by various chrysanthemum experts and it could perhaps be said that there is no room for any more. However, encouraged by the publishers, I have endeavoured to include not only present-day views of top-class growers in this country but also details from our fellow enthusiasts in many parts of the world. Some of these overseas friends were encountered when they visited our national shows in London, others are only known through the medium of correspondence, but all have one thing in common: their willingness to devote all available spare time to furthering the cause of chrysanthemum growing not only in their own countries but also internationally.

To Mrs Anne Richardson of Seattle, USA, and Mrs Shirley McMinn of Victoria, BC, Canada, whom I first met when judging at London national shows, my thanks for the hard work they have done on my behalf.

To Mrs Walter Christoffers of the National Chrysanthemum Society of America; Ken Kitney, New Zealand; Tas Jones, Bruce Furneaux and Mrs Alice Wright, Australia; Gordon Bentham and Mrs Dickson, Canada; Professor Albert Vogelmann, Munich; and Ludwig Kientzler, Germany; my grateful thanks for granting permission to use information extracted from publications of their national societies or from their own writings in describing some aspects of culture in other countries.

Nearer home, I must also record my indebtedness to the National Chrysanthemum Society of Great Britain and in particular pay tribute to its Secretary, Stanley Gosling, who spends twenty-four hours a day trying to further the cause of chrysanthemum growing.

May I finally be permitted to include a special acknowledgment to my wife who, apart from playing the not too easy role of a wife, has also given me considerable help in all my writings on the chrysanthemum.

To the many who read this book, while you may not agree with all the various methods of cultivation described, my sincere wish is that it will give a few hours enjoyment.

1 *History of the Chrysanthemum*

The exact origin of the chrysanthemum is a little obscure, but it is known to have been cultivated by man for over three thousand years. This plant was one of the earliest to be domesticated for the beauty of its flowers alone, and probably originated in China; references to chrysanthemums are found in records as early as 500 BC. Confucius, the Chinese philosopher, knew its blooms and described it in his work *Li-Ki* or *Ninth Moon* as 'the chrysanthemum with its yellow glory'. These very early flowers were wild in character and in the main yellow in colour, with a few in the mauve-pink range. They were small single flowers, very far removed from the sophisticated hybrids we know today; even the modern single cultivars have been developed and improved to such a degree that they bear little resemblance to the original chrysanthemum species.

Early Eastern influence is further confirmed by reference to a Chinese chrysanthemum specialist, T'ao-Yuan-ming (AD 365–427), who was said to be mainly responsible for many early improvements in cultural methods. Additional research reveals that a thousand years ago, Chinese poets were writing in praise of this flower, whilst replicas of chrysanthemums in their original form have been discovered on some fifteenth-century Chinese pottery. There would seem to be little doubt, therefore, as to the country of origin, even if the method of its worldwide distribution is obscure.

In a relatively short space of time, the Japanese, with their love of floriculture, realized the future potential of chrysanthemums. In the ninth century AD, imperial chrysanthemum gardens were founded by Emperor Uda where various types of chrysanthemums were gradually developed; one of these was the forerunner of our present-day large exhibition cultivars, which are still referred to as Japs by many growers. Secrets of their cultivation were jealously guarded for many centuries by workers in the Japanese royal gardens and it was not until the middle of the nineteenth century that a few plants were allowed to leave the gardens and travel to Britain. During the twelfth century, so highly regarded was the chrysanthemum that many of the mikados decorated their swords with engravings of the bloom. One mikado is said to have instituted the 'Order of Chrysanthemums' as a very high award for chivalry, which was seldom bestowed on anyone other than royalty. Finally, to set the seal on its importance in Japanese culture, in 1910 the chrysanthemum was proclaimed the national flower of Japan.

Introduction to Europe

The earliest reference to chrysanthemums in Europe is probably one made in 1689 by the botanist Bregnius and the following year a Dutch scientist named Rheede described a cultivar growing in India by the name of 'Gool-Doodi'; however, another century passed before successful cultivation took place in Europe. This happened in France in 1789, when a merchant named Pierre Louis Blancard of Marseilles brought three cultivars home from China, only one of which survived the journey and climatic change—he christened it 'Old Purple'. Eventually this cultivar reached Kew Gardens in England and its description was featured in the *Botanical Magazine* of 1796. At last the Western world, and in particular the northern hemisphere, was steadily awakening to the possibility of a considerable future for chrysanthemums. In consequence the then Horticultural Society of London, among others, gave encouragement for the importation of new cultivars from the Far East.

A great step forward was achieved in 1827, when seed was successfully produced in Europe by a retired French officer, Captain Bernet. Many previous attempts by both English and French gardeners had failed lamentably, so this date is indeed one of great historical importance in the chysanthemum world.

In 1843 the Royal Horticultural Society of London commissioned Robert Fortune to proceed on an expedition to China in search of rare plants. On his return in 1846, amongst his many finds he brought both *Chrysanthemum minimum* and Chusan daisy. The latter, it is believed, was the originator of pompoms and for many years proved to be the only chrysanthemum which would flower early enough for outdoor cultivation in the British Isles. Robert Fortune continued his interest in chrysanthemums and the first Japanese cultivars were introduced into this country by him in 1862. Of varying forms, they were known as Dragons and ranged from one best described as being similar to a garden pink to another which resembled a camellia;

none of these uncharacteristic types of chrysanthemums is known in Britain today.

The first English seedlings were raised in 1835 by Short and Free-stone, but one of the most enthusiastic English supporters of chrysanthemums was John Salter, whose name is still well known to many present-day growers. John Salter established a nursery at Versailles in France in 1838, where he produced a number of seedlings, the two most notable being 'Annie Salter' and 'Queen of England'. These both reigned supreme for over a century, being listed in the British National Chrysanthemum Register of 1960. The former was a late medium reflexed decorative, yellow in colour, while the latter was a large pale pink exhibition incurve; both were introduced in 1847. As a further point of interest, in the same register will also be found reference to the cultivar John Salter, introduced in 1866, a large red incurve (even an incurve of poor form in that colour would still be something of a novelty today).

In 1848, because of the upheaval caused by the French Revolution, John Salter was forced to return to England where he continued his interest in and improvements on chrysanthemums at a nursery in Hammersmith, London.

Another well-known raiser and distributor more than worthy of mention is Simon Delaux of Toulouse, France, who, with several other continental plantsmen, first raised those cultivars which are considered to be forerunners of the modern early-flowering decorative cultivars we know today.

America

It was not until after the beginning of the nineteenth century that the chrysanthemum was introduced into the United States. The cultivar William Penn, a new seedling at that time, was shown at the Pennsylvania Horticultural Society in 1841. At this stage chrysanthemums were only considered as garden plants, and it was not until 1860 that they also became popular in the greenhouse. For many years the chief influence in North America was from Japan, hence the predominance of spidery, quilled and other fancy cultivars grown in the USA, but larger garden and British exhibition cultivars are steadily gaining in popularity. I think it is probably true that we in Britain could well consider growing some of the more exotic types of chrysanthemums so popular in America and Japan. Bonsai cultivars, a name which up to now has been used in Britain exclusively in association with miniature trees rather than chrysanthemums, is a case in point.

Two Americans well remembered for their work in the development of cultivars in the USA are Dr Walcott and John Thorpe.

Australia

In Australia, T. W. Pockett will long be remembered for his introductions, many of which are grown extensively at the present time in Australia and are still listed in the NCS register.

Inevitably, a flower with such an historical background as the chrysanthemum was bound to gain the attention of specialist growers and this has led to the formation of national bodies in many countries which, although similar in many ways, are individually unique in their adaptation to the particular geography and ideology of the countries concerned.

National Chrysanthemum Society of Great Britain

Already better known throughout the world than any other chrysanthemum society, the British Society's international role will inevitably increase but, in common with many other organizations now held in great esteem, it arose from quite humble origins, its foundations being laid over a hundred years ago in a very small way.

In 1846, the year of Robert Fortune's return from first visiting China, this society was formed as the Borough of Hackney Chrysanthemum Society at Stoke Newington, London, and in a report of the 1852 show there is mention of blooms six inches across, which would have been considered exceedingly large in those days. The finest cultivar at this show was the previously mentioned 'Queen of England'.

Most of this society's early meetings were held at various inns with attractive names like the Amwell Arms and the Rochester Castle; I am surprised that our modern raisers do not use some of these names for their new introductions.

In 1874 the society's name was changed to the Stoke Newington and Hackney Chrysanthemum Society and three years later, in 1877, the first show was held by this very much enlarged society at the then Westminster Aquarium. A stage nearer to the present day was reached in 1884, when the society once again changed its name—this time to the one well known to all enthusiasts of today, the National Chrysanthemum Society. The society's meetings, however, were still held at an inn, the Old Four Swans at Bishopsgate in the City of London. Society exhibitions were transferred to the Crystal Palace in 1903 and carried on at that venue until 1914. This Victorian edifice, built mainly to stage exhibitions, was a landmark in south London for several decades. Many early BBC television broadcasts were transmitted from it. Sadly, although the huge building was mainly a glass and iron structure, it was destroyed by fire before the Second World War.

The first of the London national shows to be held at the Royal Horticultural Society Hall, Westminster, was in 1921, under the chairmanship of the late E. F. Hawes. The style of shows in the twenties was very different from those we see today; exhibits of multi-vase classes of large exhibition cultivars reigned supreme.

Another pioneer of our modern British National Chrysanthemum Society to whom we all owe a great deal was the late E. T. Thistle-thwaite. When he took over as a part-time Secretary in 1945, the individual membership totalled 475 and affiliated societies numbered 180; but through his continuous and dedicated hard work, on his retirement in 1959, the number of individual members had increased by monumental proportions to 9,500 and affiliated societies also to 1,400. The secretaryship was no longer a part-time job, but an extremely busy full-time one. Today, under the present Secretary, Stan Gosling, membership runs at approximately 13,000, with affiliated societies well over the 2,000 mark; there are also groups working in conjunction with the parent body in most parts of the country.

The declared object of the society is worthy of note in a condensed form: 'To promote cultivation of chrysanthemums by means of exhibitions, conferences, judges' courses and lectures and generally to do all such lawful things as are incidental or conducive to the attainment of the above object.' The term 'lawful' rather intrigues me.

American National Chrysanthemum Society Inc

In 1944 the Eastern States Chrysanthemum Society, similar to its British counterpart, started in a small way with forty members drawn from the four states of New York, New Jersey, Pennsylvania and Connecticut. By 1945 membership had increased to 198, spread over thirty-three states, and in 1946 the present name of National Chrysan-themum Society Inc, usa, was adopted. The late Dr Ernest Lyman Scott, to whom the current American Show and Judges Handbook is dedicated, was the founder of the American society and I should like to quote the last line from the dedication which appears in this handbook (No 6): 'To those of us who knew him, Ernest Lyman Scott was truly a man among men.' Such a tribute cannot be bettered by anyone.

Present-day membership is already well over 3,000 and still rising rapidly but with such a vast continent and variation in weather con-ditions it is obviously not so easy to concentrate activities as it is in Britain. Many aspects of growing, because of varying latitudes, differ far more than they do in Britain, but two points of comparison be-tween the British and American societies will be of interest to readers from both countries.

Apart from individual members in Great Britain, there are only affiliated societies and no rules are laid down regarding the number of NCS members that a society must have in order to apply for affiliation. In America, however, there are conditions to be met before affiliation can be obtained. There are two forms of association with the national body. Chapter societies must consist of not less than ten persons and all their members, irrespective of the total number, must also be mem-bers of the national body. An affiliated society, however, whilst it must include not less than ten members of the national body, can also have additional members of its society who are not national members; but only a chapter society is given the privilege of staging a National Chrysanthemum Society annual show and advertising it as a show sponsored by the national body. In this way membership of the national body is encouraged. I would suggest that there is something that we in Britain could learn from this; it must mean that the national body is kept alive by all its members' views and not only perhaps the odd few.

Finally, the definition of the objects of the American society is less formal than ours: 'The objectives of the society are to improve the standard of excellence of the chrysanthemum, to promote a wider interest in the cultivation of the chrysanthemum, to encourage a greater use and display of the beautiful blooms of the many cultivars of the chrysanthemum and to increase the bond of fellowship between the growers of the chrysanthemum.'

Other National Societies

There are also to be found in New Zealand, Australia and Japan national societies which, although operating on a much smaller scale than British society, still have the same enthusiasm and are just as keen. I feel sure that, with increasing interchange of views and ideas, the day is not so far distant when we shall see a world chrysanthemum conference at regular intervals.

2 Classification by Type and Season

With such a depth of historical background, it is not surprising that a great many gardeners have resorted to growing chrysanthemums in order to help relieve the tensions of modern living; it must be strongly emphasized that it is not necessary to become a fanatical exhibitor to succeed in this endeavour. Many people are still under the impression that to produce good blooms it is necessary to use secret potions, to utter incantations over plants in the dead of night, and perhaps, just to make sure, give massive doses of fertilizers. This type of witchcraft, as we progress through the different aspects of cultivation, will be seen to be completely unnecessary and wrong; although there is no doubt that chrysanthemums do need a little more care than many other occupants of the garden or greenhouse, cultivation does not have to become an obsession to succeed. The only thing I will admit to doing other than treating my chyrsanthemums as ordinary plants is talking to them, but not always, I am afraid, in a complimentary manner. They do not seem to object to my criticisms and bravely carry on to bloom in their beauty as if to prove me wrong. I would stress from the outset that my intention has been to give all the various stages of cultivation in detail in the belief that keen gardeners are always seeking information that increases knowledge about their hobby. It does not mean that all the intricate steps have to be followed, but it is very necessary, indeed essential, to have such information available should it be required.

Basis of Classification

The chrysanthemum belongs to the same plant family as the common daisy, botanically known as the Compositae or composites because its bloom combines two separate but closely related floral systems. In the centre, visible in the single type of bloom but not usually visible in the double cultivars, is a cushion of small bisexual disk florets, both male and female, either yellow or green in colour.

Around this central disk are long unisexual female florets which are often wrongly referred to as petals; these have many varying colours and forms.

These characteristics of the bloom are used as the basis for determining its classification by combining shape, size, manner in which the ray florets grow and whether or not the disk florets are normally visible. The terms used to describe the various floral types of chrysanthemums basically do not change in most countries. The number used to indicate the appropriate classification does vary.

In this chapter we are more concerned with actual form descriptions.

INCURVED

The chief characteristic of incurves, which are looked upon by many growers as the aristocrats of the chrysanthemum world, is the firm neat form which gives a completely globular appearance. The florets are placed close to each other, tightly incurved, and may range from very thin to quite broad, but on no account must these blooms show an open centre. Their handicap for use in garden decoration is that, because florets incurve, rain is trapped and runs into the centre of the bloom where it finds difficulty in draining away. The incurved form is found in the early-flowering outdoor types and also in the late greenhouse section under the heading of exhibition incurves. The American classification extends this to describing the different large exhibition cultivars, when appropriate, as incurves.

REFLEXED

These are completely opposite to the incurves, as their florets turn outwards and downwards from a central tuft of florets so that the shape can, in most cases, be likened to an umbrella. Because of this form they are far more suitable for growing in the open garden, as the rain runs off the bloom rather than into it. A reflexed bloom is far more versatile than any other chyrsanthemum as it can be used equally well for all purposes. If left unrestricted the resulting sprays are attractive and many of the late cultivars, such as the 'Princess Anne' family, lend themselves to commercial production of dwarf pot plants. They are also found in the late decorative section and once more in the American classification for large exhibition.

If I had to pick on one particular type of chrysanthemum for the new grower, I would recommend the medium reflexed cultivars without hesitation.

INTERMEDIATE

As indicated by the American classification of this type of bloom as reflexing incurves, they are neither wholly incurved nor wholly reflexed. Often they follow a similar pattern to that of incurved blooms, except that the florets are very much looser and do not fully close over at the top. They can also have the top half of the bloom incurving whilst the bottom reflexes, giving a skirting effect.

POMPONS AND SEMI-POMPONS

These small double flowers, about 20mm ($\frac{3}{4}$in) in diameter, are either spherical or half-spherical in shape. They should never be disbudded as they rely upon their beauty as bushy plants covered in flowers. These are definitely the ideal subject for garden border decoration. Their ease of cultivation will particularly appeal to the keen gardener who requires good results from very little work. The height of growth varies from approximately 30cm to 60cm (about 1–2ft) and if plants are placed in groups of about six, fairly close together, they will merge into one another thus making a beautiful cushion of colour. Most cultivars are of the early-flowering types which normally flower in this country before frosts come at the end of October or early November. The cultivar 'Denise', a good yellow, seems to be a universally well-known example of this splendid type of chrysanthemum, though there are many more delightful names and cultivars available.

SPRAYS

These cultivars are grown in a natural manner so that, instead of having only one large bloom to a stem and restricting the number of stems, there are many flowers on a branched stem. Most early-flowering cultivars will grow well as sprays but in addition there are many early and late cultivars, both single and double blooms, which are marketed especially for this purpose by many nurserymen. In America sprays are catered for to a much greater extent and form an integral part of the show programme. American classification of these, unlike the British, is divided into three different classes, namely, standard terminal spray, acceptable terminal spray and crown spray.

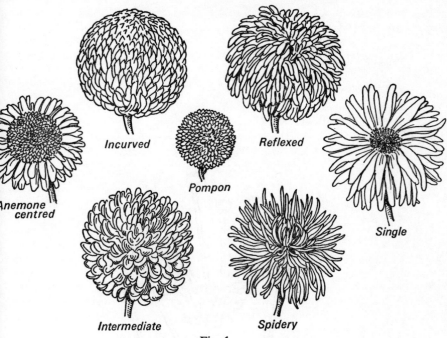

Fig. 1

THE BASIS OF CHRYSANTHEMUM CLASSIFICATION

Type of Bloom	Early Flowering	October Flowering	Late Flowering
Incurved (tight globe)	23	13	3
Reflexed (like an umbrella)	24	14	4
Intermediate (in between, loosely incurved or not fully reflexed)	25	15	5
Anemone (pin-cushion centre)	26	–	6
Pompon (small ball-shaped blooms)	28	18	8
Single (daisy-like showing centre disk)	27	17	7
Spray (unrestricted mass of smaller blooms)	29	19	9
Any other types	30	20	10 Spidery 11 Other

The numbers refer to sections according to formation of blooms

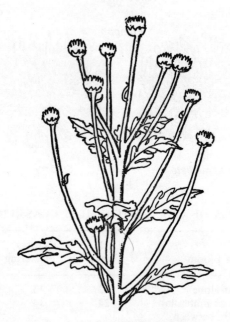

Fig. 2 Perfect terminal spray

The crown spray, which has no disbudding, is not considered to be of show quality and its exhibition at chapter shows is discouraged. This classification would appear to be the spray as we know it in Britain, but to explain all the intricate details of American sprays and the judging of them would take a small book in itself; interested readers are advised to obtain the American Show and Judges Handbook (see Appendix D).

ANEMONE-CENTRED

These single, daisy-like flowers have a large central cushion of disk florets which are tube-like and elongated, forming a very prominent disk which can best be described as having a central pincushion effect similar in appearance to the annual scabious. From this disk extend short ray florets, often of a contrasting colour.

SINGLES

These are the simple daisy-type flowers with ray florets varying from a single row up to approximately five rows which radiate from the central yellow or green disk, usually grown as lates, flowering in the greenhouse. There are a few early-flowering cultivars, but there seems to be very little demand for them.

SPIDERY

These flowers have long-quilled florets, the most popular one in Britain being 'Rayonnante' and its various coloured sports. There are many more cultivars in commerce which are very popular with the ladies for floral decoration purposes.

On a recent tour of Britain, members of the American NCS expressed surprise at the London National Show that in Britain we do not grow and show spiders, quilled and spoon cultivars and the less common lacinated and brush-like types which are all such a feature of their growing calendars. However, it is very doubtful if these cultivars could ever replace what to us are our normal cultivars.

CHARMS

Mostly cultivated as decorative pot plants to flower from October onwards, these can be grown from seed sown in February or March or else taken as cuttings from named cultivars at about the same time. They make wonderful specimen plants, often having 2–3,000 small blooms similar in form to the blooms of small Michaelmas daisies.

CASCADES

These are flowering plants like miniature waterfalls, with hundreds of blooms. Although very attractive they are not grown very frequently by amateurs, but are nearly always seen in displays presented by parks departments at the major shows.

This completes what might be termed specialist kinds of chrysanthemums, which I shall be dealing with in detail, but the popularity of this wonderful flower is also dependent upon many other members of the chrysanthemum genus which are easy to grow and consequently are ideal subjects for the herbaceous border—indeed, many gardeners will possibly not know that they are of the same genus. It will therefore be appropriate to mention these before proceeding to the seasonal classification.

EASY-TO-GROW BORDER CHRYSANTHEMUMS

Annual chrysanthemum (*C. carinatum*)   Grown from seed each year, these are half-hardy annuals, single in form, with distinct rings of various colours which make them very pleasing border plants.

Chrysanthemum maximum   This is a perennial plant that can be increased in borders by division, commonly known as the Shasta daisy or King Edward daisy. There are several cultivars such as 'Esther Read' and 'Everest', both white in colour.

Chrysanthemum rubellum   Another perennial with purple-pink flowers similar in appearance to a Michaelmas daisy, this is very useful for massing in borders.

Korean hybrids   This is a very hardy strain of small singles and semi-doubles, which can be left out all the winter. With the NCS classification, as cultivars are classified by flower types, Koreans will be either singles, pompons or sprays as the case may be.

Marguerites or Paris daisy (*C. frutescens*)   This small-flowered plant is extensively used for window box culture.

Pyrethrum   These are among the most useful of border plants. They are mainly single in form and are found in a variety of colours. Since they dislike drought conditions it is important that adequate watering is given during very dry spells. Having a daisy-like form, they are often said to rival the single-flowered autumn chrysanthemum. Recently a few double types of pyrethrum have also been marketed and possibly more of these will be available in a few years' time.

Seasonal Classification

In a compact country like Britain it is comparatively simple to segregate the various cultivars into clearly defined seasons; there may be a difference of a week or ten days in the production of the mature bloom in any given season for a particular cultivar grown in the extreme south as compared with Scotland. This time of flowering can easily be manipulated by an alteration in the date cuttings are taken and the stopping given.

The National Chrysanthemum Society has found over the years that time of flowering linked to normal methods of growing gives three definite convenient periods in which blooms are brought to maturity. These are: early-flowering plants which normally bloom before 1 October; October-flowering; and the lates which are flowered in greenhouses during the months of November, December and January. Possibly we are fortunate in this respect, compared with countries like Australia and America. For example it is found that in the New York area, cuttings purchased from a nursery in California must have an allowance of approximately fourteen days more than the flowering dates given in the catalogue to compensate for the difference in latitude.

EARLY-FLOWERING

Cultivars in this group are grown in the open and flower before 1 October. Protection is allowed for show purposes and can be given by the erection of covers, using greaseproof bags or other methods and there is no reason why these cannot be grown as pot plants if you wish, although this is rather pointless when culture in the open ground is so much easier. The ordinary gardener growing for garden decoration or cut-flowers can, without much trouble, expect this section to flower during the period from late July to early October.

OCTOBER-FLOWERING

These are chiefly what could be termed later versions of the early-flowering blooms which can be grown in the open ground if you live in an area which does not suffer from early frosts or, if required, they can be treated as lates and flowered in a greenhouse. For exhibition, this group is allowed to be shown at both early and late shows in their respective classes. In fact, with few exceptions, they are not recommended for exhibition work as, being natural October-flowering cultivars, it is necessary either to advance the flowering time to stage at the September shows or to delay flowering for the late shows in November. This interference usually means that nature, in its own way, objects and the blooms are often not as good as one would wish.

LATE GREENHOUSE TYPES

The decoratives and exhibition incurved cultivars are similar to the early-flowering versions. The main difference is that they will flower in pots in a greenhouse during early November or December, while a few cultivars will carry over into January should you want your blooms to decorate your home in the bare winter months.

Large and medium exhibition cultivars are purely exhibition blooms, being much too large for any other use. Personally I do not know of any other type of show bench chrysanthemum more attractive than a multi-vase class for these very spectacular monsters. They offer every challenge possible to obtain perfection and the number of good growers in this field is probably far less than for any other type. Many may not agree with me, but to have shown Japs successfully, even at local shows, is, I think, the hallmark of successful chrysanthemum growing.

Singles are a very different proposition. Although a great deal of experience and knowledge is required to produce good blooms, they can at least be grown in most cases with four to eight good blooms per plant depending on the cultivar. The drawback is that far too many of them grow over 2 metres (7ft) in height and this can lead to complications at housing time if you are not prepared for it. I well remember years ago, when I first started growing lates, my first greenhouse was quite small and not all that high; fortunately I had only laid a central concrete path, so I was able to dig out some of the earth and lower pots. This was all right immediately after housing but the trouble was that as stems continued to grow, I had to burrow underneath and eventually finished with one pot sunk well into the ground whilst the blooms stuck out through an open roof ventilator. There was a happy ending in that they won a first award at a local show; ironically, the name of the cultivar was 'Mayford Giant'.

From this I learnt two things which I must pass on to any beginner with lates. First of all, find out heights of cultivars before purchasing them, and here do not rely only upon the catalogue height of the nurseryman who, when he gives the height of a cultivar, really means it will be at least half as high again. Second, make sure your greenhouse is tall enough to allow for a height of 2¾ metres (approx 9ft) as this is really essential for successful late cultivation.

Anemone-centred cultivars, like singles, are highly decorative but are not as yet seen very frequently. Their popularity may increase greatly if there is sufficient demand for them, especially by ladies interested in floral art.

This, then, is the main classification of the chrysanthemum in Britain at the present time. There may well be changes in the future, but before this comes about to any major degree, undoubtedly there will have to be a considerable amount of international co-operation to cater for other varying types which up to now I have only mentioned briefly with reference to other countries.

Colour Classification

It would be quite impossible to have sufficient colour classifications to cover all the varying degrees of the range of colours. It is therefore necessary to compromise to some extent, though personally I would like to see one or two more colours included to give a better indication. It is admitted that the intention is merely to give a general guide to gardeners and nurserymen in their catalogues, but to me it seems wrong that a borderline cream cultivar should be called white or pale yellow; similarly, there would appear to be a need to indicate another shade of deep pink to cover the present ranges from pink and purple. It is possible that an extension of three or four more colours may be made to deal with this problem in the not too distant future.

The present official NCS classification is as follows:

B	Bronze	R	Red
LB	Light bronze	W	White
P	Pink	Y	Yellow
PP	Pale pink	PY	Pale yellow
S	Salmon	O	Other colours (this covers such colours as green and oyster shades)
Pu	Purple		

To summarize my conclusions from this colour chart, I would like to see a classification to cover the orange stage between yellow and bronze; deep pink between pink and purple; cream, which at the moment is allocated to pale yellow; and crimson to indicate the dark velvet red colour as opposed to the normal red. This would not cause any complications in show schedules catering for colour classes, but would certainly help to give a much better indication to the ordinary gardener looking through the catalogues.

3 Effects of Light and Temperature on Growth

Commercial growers have long appreciated the combined effects of light and temperature on chrysanthemums and have used these under controlled conditions to produce blooms and pot plants all the year round on a very large scale. The keen gardener, while not concerned with this method of cultivation, has possibly realized that the influence of these two media does have a distinct role in producing blooms of quality.

For my purpose, I like to consider the plant in two separate compartments: firstly the root system or power house below soil level and secondly vegetative growth above ground which I liken to the factory conveyor belt producing the end product, which in this case is the bloom. The first real and considerable effect of temperature occurs in what is known as vernalization, when plants are practically dormant during the winter—an elaborate name no doubt, but in simple terms it means subjecting the root of the plant to a period of cold conditions lasting for at least a month. During this time a temperature not exceeding 7°C (45°F) is very necessary; failure to give this period of vernalization is likely to result in cuttings taken for propagation purposes which give either rosetted growth or premature buds on very short stems at an early stage. It is true that all cultivars do not necessarily require this treatment, particularly those specially bred and used for growing all-the-year-round plants in pots when a constant temperature of 15°C (60°F) is maintained, but to be on the safe side, the amateur grower would be well advised to maintain a vernalization period on all cultivars used for cut-flower, garden decoration and exhibition purposes. The effects of temperature on vegetative growth and bud initiation is that under low temperatures, development is slower with a consequent delay in budding and flowering. Nature in her wisdom has, in a reasonably normal season, arranged for a steady increase of temperature during spring until mid-summer, followed by a decrease through autumn to early winter. The chrysanthemum has adapted itself to this rise and fall in temperature and although short days are essential for proper bud development, an additional factor is that a minimum night temperature of 15°C (60°F) during the early days of bud formation is highly desirable; as the bud becomes visible, this night temperature should fall to 10–13°C (50–55°F). Although seldom completely achieved, these figures are the ideal, as high temperatures invariably lead to lack of size and intensity of colour in blooms; but quite obviously most of us are at the mercy of the elements. This does, however, explain some of the reasons why, depending upon the season, blooms may be early or late, often lacking in size, and sometimes completely out of character from the usual expected development of a particular cultivar.

As if this were not enough to make things difficult, we have the additional effects of the intensity of light on the plants from the time cuttings are taken until the production of mature blooms. Chrysanthemums are known as 'short day' plants and buds will only develop satisfactorily when day length has been reduced to approximately fourteen hours; it might possibly be more accurate to describe the chrysanthemum as a 'long night' plant, but this effect of light and hours of darkness, although so important, is not the only effect of light which must be considered. Another reason why good light is necessary during the earlier stages of vegetative growth is that on bright days the leaves will not only manufacture sufficient plant sugars for the immediate well-being of the plant but will also store an excess as a reserve. During dull days, sugar produced will probably be only sufficient for the plant's current needs and no surplus will be available to store as a reserve supply. From this it will be seen that a reasonable level of light is necessary to ensure the proper development of the bud and later of the bloom; lack of light will automatically lead to smaller blooms at flowering time and while this may not unduly worry an enthusiastic gardener, to the exhibitor in these days of keen competition, this lack of size will be the difference between success and failure. Taken a stage further, the need to plant early-flowering cultivars in as open a position as possible to ensure maximum light becomes increasingly more obvious. The summer standing ground for late-flowering cultivars should also be in as open a position as possible but here, unlike earlies, steps can be taken after housing by adjusting temperature to counteract any ill effects which may have resulted through lack of light. Experiments have shown that night temperatures affect the plant's response to the length of day much more than day temperatures. This once more stresses the importance of the hours or darkness upon chrysanthemum development.

Although I have only touched on the very fringe of this complicated subject, it must be remembered that it is not only the single effect of light or temperature which affects the growth and flowering for most cultivars, but rather a combination of the two which gives the right conditions. To benefit from this knowledge it is very necessary to keep complete records over several seasons; the information thus gained will assist in the understanding of the plant's needs together with their surroundings and this must inevitably lead to better blooms.

4 *Soil and Compost*

Soil

To many growers of chrysanthemums, soil is casually dismissed as being a medium in which roots of plants are anchored, yet the success of our hobby is so dependent upon this wonderful gift which has been given to us by nature that as such, it surely is entitled to more respect and certainly worthy of mention here in more detail.

Originating from the weathering and disintegration of rocks forming the earth's crust thousands of years ago, it is the top 60cm (2ft) of soil in which we are mostly interested. It is true that roots of trees and other plants often penetrate to depths of 2 or 3 metres (6–9ft) to obtain firmer anchorage; nevertheless, most chrysanthemums, under natural conditions, confine their root systems to the top 30cm (12in) of soil. Using intensive cultivation conditions produced by regular attention and constant addition of humus-forming materials, root activity can be greatly extended into the second 30cm (12in) of soil—one reason for double digging.

The tendency of plant roots to keep near to the surface is mostly attributable to the fact that soil is warmer near the surface during the growing season; it also contains more oxygen, so necessary for proper root development.

The physical structure of soil is governed by particle size, water content, nutrient retention properties and temperature. The three divisions of particle size are sand, silt and clay; sand again can be subdivided into coarse or fine, with varying in-between stages. Whilst any soil contains particles of different sizes, usually one size range will predominate and it is this particular size which governs whether the soil is termed light, medium or heavy. Small particles will bind tightly together, excluding much air and, with moisture filling a large proportion of the remaining air space, the result is heavy soil. The reverse applies with soil containing larger particles, giving sandy or light conditions. This is a basic description of soil but it cannot be said to be fertile unless it has an additional supply of air and water. If it contains water without air, then the soil becomes heavy and waterlogged; very little, other than marsh or bog plants will grow under these conditions. On the other hand, all air and no water results in very difficult growing conditions associated with sand and gravel during periods of drought; artificial watering on its own has little chance of curing this defect. These difficulties can be minimized and eventually overcome by the use of manures and bulky organic materials such as peat, garden compost, wool shoddy or spent hops. These help to open heavy soils while light soils are assisted in retaining their moisture.

Certain fertilizers will also help to correct soils so that they produce better crops. For example, lime is often used to break down heavy clay soils and nitrate of soda or muriate of potash helps to bind lighter soils; but I leave the specific subject of fertilizers to be dealt with more fully in the next section on fertilizers and their uses.

There is another aspect of soil which has a great effect on the production of good chrysanthemums, this is the reaction to tests for acidity or alkalinity which is identified by the letters pH followed by a number. The scale runs from a neutral point of pH7 to pH14 for absolute alkalinity, while in the other direction pH0 indicates complete acidity; this means a reading of pH6 is slightly acid and pH8 is slightly alkaline. In practice it has been found that the best chrysanthemums are usually produced in a soil having a very slight acid reaction of pH6·5, so it is very necessary to have regular soil tests making sure of the actual pH value; steps can then be taken to correct any excessive degree of acidity of alkalinity to keep the soil at this required level.

It will readily be appreciated from these comments that all soils have an inherent degree of fertility but, unless we replenish the humus and food used by plants with the addition of bulky organic materials and fertilizers, the fertility and physical structure will gradually deteriorate and the soil will become exhausted, in consequence of which plants will soon show their natural objections to these poor conditions. Suitable manures and fertilizers are dealt with more fully in chapter 5.

POTTING COMPOST MATERIALS

It is possible to mix your own compost, provided a good supply of medium loam, peat and coarse sand is available, but there are few

gardeners who have proper facilities to mix all the necessary ingredients thoroughly. Personally I still prefer to buy my supplies ready-
mixed and although it is said that much of the compost sold these
days is of inferior quality, fortunately it is still possible to find a
good source of supply at a reasonable price. However, if you wish to
mix your own compost the following advice should be of some help.

Loam

The first essential is to obtain good medium loam. Loam prepared
with fibrous turves cut from well-drained pasture land, having a
pH value of 6·5, is probably the best medium for good compost
making. The turves should be approximately 10cm (4in) thick and
are usually supplied 30cm (12in) wide by 1 metre (1 yard) in length.
They need to be stacked carefully, grass side downwards, and
watered well if dry. A sprinkling of lime plus a 5-cm (2-in) layer of
well-rotted manure in between alternate layers of turves will help the
loam to give that little extra body so liked by chrysanthemums. A
wise precaution is to sprinkle each layer with insecticide powder to
destroy any soil pests that may be present. Wire worms can be particularly troublesome in turves.

It is recognized that the most effective results are obtained if the
stack is not larger than approximately 2 metres (6ft) square and
1½ metres (4½ft) high, and it is stacked in early summer for use the
following year. When required for use, after skimming off the outer
layer of the stack, the remainder will need to be riddled or finely
chopped; the coarser residue can be kept on one side to be incorporated in the next stack.

Peat

Peat, used in various types of composts, is also a very important
ingredient; as with soil, it can be variable in quality depending upon
the type of vegetation from which it was formed. Sedge peat is
probably the best for chrysanthemum composts, although any good
granular peat can be used. It is more economical to buy in a bale
rather than loose, but it must be broken down and given a number of
waterings until it is moist right through; to use peat in a dry state
will mean that moisture will be absorbed by the peat to the detriment of the young roots of plants. Any nutrients contained in peat
are so small that they can be completely ignored, but this can be

considered a good thing as fertilizers can always be added at required strengths with a much greater degree of control than is possible with the unknown food value in manure.

Sand

A good-quality sand is as vital to a well-mixed compost as any other of the main ingredients, indeed it is possibly just a fraction more important. Without sand, compost will not keep open and the consequent exclusion of air will hinder adequate root development because of the tendency to waterlogging.

To perform its function correctly, the sand must be coarse and sharp; grading up to 3mm ($\frac{1}{8}$ in) is usually recommended. It is no good using fine silver or potting sand.

John Innes Compost

The famous compost devised by the John Innes Insitute after very intensive research and experimentation has now become a household name. I could perhaps be accused of being old-fashioned, but I think it is the most suitable compost for chrysanthemum culture ranging from the propagation of cuttings to final potting of late cultivars,

The standard compost known as No 1 is extremely good for striking cuttings and is made up in the following manner, great care being taken to measure the quantities of fertilizers accurately.

7 seed trays loam
3 seed trays moist peat
2 seed trays coarse sand

Using a standard seed tray 35cm × 21cm × 7$\frac{1}{2}$cm (14in × 8$\frac{1}{2}$in × 3in) deep. This will give approx 73 litres (2 bushels) of compost.

To this bulk of compost are added:

80g (3oz) hoof and horn
80g (3oz) superphosphate of lime
40g (1$\frac{1}{2}$oz) sulphate of potash
40g (1$\frac{1}{2}$oz) ground chalk or ground limestone

The peat, in a well-moistened condition, is first mixed thoroughly with the loam; then the fertilizers are mixed with the ground chalk and sand in a dry condition. The sand mixture is then added to the peat-loam mixture and the whole is turned several times to make sure the fertilizers are evenly distributed.

It is now possible to buy the three fertilizers mixed to the above quantities as John Innes base fertilizer from any horticultural sundriesman. Thus 200g (7½oz) of John Innes base plus the 40g (1½oz) of ground chalk are needed for our 2 bushels of compost. By doubling, trebling or quadrupling the amount of fertilizer we have John Innes No 2, 3 or 4 mixtures respectively. No 2 mixture is suitable for potting or boxing on chrysanthemum cuttings once rooted and it can also be used as a layer in a cold frame about 10 cm (4in) deep, for direct planting of cuttings from their propagating boxes. No 3 is recommended for potting on into 12½ or 15cm (5 or 6in) pots while the No 4 mixture, with its higher food value, is excellent for the final potting of late-flowering cultivars as the compost will be rich enough in food content to last for three or four weeks after potting.

Many growers consider that a modified version of the John Innes formula containing slightly more loam and a little less peat and sand gives better results. This is really a question of individual experimentation but whatever the modifications are, the total bulk of materials used should remain the same for the recommended amount of fertilizers.

Soil-less Compost

In recent years the popularity of soil-less compost has come well to the fore for several reasons. In some areas a shortage of good loam for making the conventional soil compost has often been such that alternatives have been welcome. I do not fully agree with the supposed shortage of loam as any really keen grower will soon find a source of supply for anything connected with his hobby; however, to be in this category he must be completely devoted to his hobby in contrast to the normally keen grower who expects supplies to be fairly easily obtained. Soil-less composts are now available at most general horticultural sundries shops. They are sold well-packaged in polythene bags or sacks and are of a very uniform standard. Levington compost is possibly the best-known of the soil-less media but it is quite possible to make your own.

There are obviously many different theories as to exactly how the various ingredients should be mixed. Suffice it to say that most of them are very successful but to avoid the rather tedious task of measuring out small quantities of various fertilizers for mixing with the main bulk, most growers prefer to use a proprietary fertilizer. In the formula now given I have used Phostrogen, as I have found this to be excellent for the purpose; however, it must be emphasized that many other well-known fertilizers will give equally good results although, as with most phases of chrysanthemum culture, some experimentation may be required to find out the best quantities.

To prepare the compost, mix three parts by volume of well-moistened peat with one part by volume of sharp sand and when they have been very thoroughly mixed, add Phostrogen at the rate of 80g (3oz) per bushel with a further 80g (3oz) of ground chalk. This compost will be suitable for taking cuttings, also for potting into $7\frac{1}{2}$ or 9cm (3 or $3\frac{1}{2}$in) pots without any further feed. Once the plants are potted on into larger pots, some additional feeding will need to be given in a liquid form after about two weeks has elapsed. Over the years, experience gained in using soil-less composts as a growing medium has bought to light several distinct features which are different from the conventional methods used with the John Innes composts. Cuttings rooted in soil-less composts produce a strong root system very much more quickly than in a soil compost. This continues after plants are boxed or potted on and, consequently, a later start in taking cuttings should be made, seven to fourteen days being the average period of delay.

The nutrient value of most peat composts is much lower than the John Innes No 4 compost used for final potting; therefore, instead of waiting approximately one month before commencing supplementary feeding, it is better to start with a liquid feed and to continue to do this at practically every watering after two weeks of final potting. Watering must be studied, taking care to see that the compost is never allowed to dry right out. In dry sunny weather, pots will dry out more quickly than with soil composts, but in dull, cloudy weather, the drying-out process will take a little longer. When water is needed it must be given in a sufficient quantity to make sure the whole of the pot is moist right through. Here the axiom must be: if in doubt, water—the complete opposite of everything which has been taught with soil composts where, if there was any doubt, the grower has always been advised to wait until the next day.

When potting in a peat compost, the old conventional rammer must be discarded. Nothing more than finger firming is necessary so that the compost will still be fairly loose. This will present some difficulty with final potting when the cane is inserted as, if left unsupported, it will not be firm; this must therefore be fastened to a strainer wire immediately. With continuous watering during the season, the medium should have been firmed enough by the time plants are housed to hold the cane, although with some cultivars it may still be necessary to give extra support in the greenhouse. Better to be safe than sorry and spoil a whole year's work.

One final word of advice: if you have had experience with soil composts such as John Innes, you will need to forget most of what you have learned and start again from scratch. The new grower should have no problems if he follows the advice given for peat composts right from the very beginning.

5 Manures and Fertilizers

To obtain chrysanthemums with well-formed blooms of good size and colour, ranging from large specialist exhibition blooms to charming sprays for garden decoration or cut-flowers, requires intelligent use of manures and fertilizers. The multitude of substances which can be used may bewilder newcomers to chrysanthemum culture unless some explanation and guidance is given.

Many nutrients are supplied to plants from the atmosphere and also from the effects of light on their foliage, but most of the necessary nourishment is obtained by the application of bulky organic matter, concentrated organic fertilizers and also concentrated mineral or artificial fertilizers added to the soil.

Chrysanthemums have almost equal needs for nitrogen (N), phosphoric acid (P_2O_5) and potash (K_2O), which are all in varying degrees supplied by these manures and fertilizers. An additional class of specialized substances known as trace elements also supply minute quantities of minerals not normally found in ordinary fertilizers. These are dealt with at the end of this section for use by the more dedicated grower.

Bulky Organic Manures

The chief feature of organic manures is that they contain a large bulk of organic matter, and although nutrient substances are present in varying degrees, for our purpose these can be ignored; in effect we rely mainly on this organic material to supply our humus material. When more concentrated fertilizers are applied, because of the presence of ample humus, they will more easily and readily be transformed into a suitable chemical state to be absorbed and used as food by plants.

Apart from the effect of humus in the soil, bulky organic matter will also help condition light soils to retain moisture and, obversely, greatly assist in the breaking down of heavy clay soil so necessary for good cultivation.

FARMYARD MANURE

This product can vary considerably, depending upon the age and health of the animals and the kind of litter that has been used in stalls and stables. Straw bedding is much the best but, except in country areas, it is doubtful if straw will have been used; coarse peat, wood shavings and bracken are all more commonly used. Unfortunately, because any kind of farmyard manure is at a premium these days, few gardeners can afford to be selective. It is always as well before buying to inspect manure and ensure that you are not paying the top price for straw manure and being supplied with an inferior product containing ninety per cent wood shavings, so often the predominant feature of manure offered for sale by street traders who knock on your door on a Sunday morning. Pig manure, if well-rotted, is possibly superior to anything else in the field of organic material for chrysanthemums. It does, however, have one severe drawback, even when well rotted: its pungent smell makes it exceedingly difficult to use and keep the peace with neighbours. The fortunate householder with several acres of ground may possibly not be worried, as the growing site can be well away from the house, but the vast majority of small semi-detached house occupants will find it is practically impossible to use pig manure, no matter how dedicated they may become to gardening and chrysanthemum growing in particular, because of their close proximity to other houses.

One of the greatest problems facing any gardener is to decide how often manure should be applied. A soil test for humus and fertilizer content is the only sure way to ascertain the answer to this question, but it is one thing to give advice and quite another to take it; speaking from experience, a very small percentage of gardeners will go to the trouble of having a soil test each year. In the absence of a test my advice would be that, once ground has been brought into good heart, you apply a dressing of manure when digging every second year. Many experts recommend incorporating manure every year, but this may lead to other failures which can be likened to indigestion in human beings through eating too much good food.

One final word of warning: never use manure which is too fresh

3 Late-flowering cultivars ready for taking cuttings

1 (Previous page, above) *Left*: tip cutting; *centre*: normal cutting; *right*: basal shoot ready to prepare for a cutting

2 (Previous page, below) Stools of early flowering cultivars ready for taking cuttings

4 Planting out

5 Standing ground for lates during summer

6 Final potting, with pot ready to receive plants

7 Late-flowering plant ready to move to final pot

8 Placing bag over bud

9 Bagging completed

and not rotted properly, as this will literally burn roots of young plants when they are planted out, with devastating results.

COMPOST

It is doubtful if any garden produces sufficient waste material suitable for composting but by supplementing kitchen and garden waste with straw, spent hops, leaves or any material capable of rotting, it is surprising how much humus can be ploughed back into the soil each year. Only if the ingredients used are well-rotted can good compost be obtained; logically, therefore, the construction of a compost heap must be very carefully carried out. Some years ago, a compost pit was always recommended by writers and lecturers, but this did not necessarily lead to its contents being well-rotted as often it became waterlogged. It is therefore advisable to build above soil level, allowing air to circulate through the heap thus assisting the biological processes which help rotting down. Using a compost accelerator will be quick and far more efficient and whatever reagent is used as the accelerator, it usually supplies nitrogen and potash as nutrients in a readily available form and calcium as a corrective against acidity which may develop in the compost heap. This property of the reagent will more than counteract the fact that a high proportion of material used in composting tends to be poor in mineral salts and nitrogen, as invariably the richest parts of plants have been utilized by us in satisfying food or in other ways before they are placed on the compost heap.

PEAT

Decayed vegetable matter which has been decomposed by water contains few if any nutrients, but as a supplier of humus it can hardly be rivalled. Many ardent chrysanthemum growers, simply because of this lack of nutrient content as opposed to farmyard manure, prefer to use peat supplemented by a feeding programme which can be controlled from the outset. No chemical analysis is necessary to determine the nutrients present as in the case of farmyard manures. In every other respect, peat is incorporated into the soil in the same manner as manure. The only precaution that must be observed is to ensure the peat is in a thoroughly moist condition before it is dug in, otherwise it will take many months to absorb the necessary moisture, to the detriment of the surrounding soil and, in turn, any plants in the close vicinity.

OTHER ORGANIC MANURES

There are a number of other very suitable manures and humus-forming materials which can be used and which are easily obtainable provided a source of supply is within reasonable distance of the grower. These vary in different parts of the country, often depending upon local industry or environment. Wool shoddy in Yorkshire or Lancashire, seaweed near the coast, poultry manure in country areas and spent hops from breweries are just a few of the commodities which can be utilized. I have no doubt that in Britain, as well as America, Australia and New Zealand, there are probably many other materials of a similar nature that are used. One well-known Australian raiser of new cultivars even finds crushed polystyrene has its uses for successful chrysanthemum culture, in conditioning his chrysanthemum beds and compost used for final potting.

Concentrated Organic Fertilizers

Mostly obtained from waste products of animal carcasses, these fertilizers are marketed after processing in either powder or granulated form. They are very popular and safer to use than concentrated artificial fertilizers. In a coarse form, their effects are more gradual, releasing various nutrients over a long period, which facilitates application to soil when preparing ground early in the year prior to planting out. If used in conjunction with bulky manure, it is possible to supply practically all the nutrients required for a whole season at this time, though it must be admitted that exhibitors will practice supplementary feeding during the season in the continuous efforts to produce blooms of better size and quality.

HOOF AND HORN MEAL (NITROGEN 13–14%)

As the name implies, this is a product from slaughterhouses and is used because of its steady supply of nitrogen. The degree of fineness achieved in the grinding down process determines how quickly nitrogen is released. A fine grade is probably the most beneficial in chrysanthemum growing, and is best applied when final preparation of the ground is made.

DRIED BLOOD (NITROGEN 11–13%)

Another nitrogenous fertilizer, dried blood is much quicker in action than hoof and horn, which makes it very suitable to help give plants a boost shortly after planting out.

BONEMEAL (NITROGEN 3·5–4%, INSOLUBLE PHOSPHORIC ACID 19%)

Bonemeal contains a high proportion of phosphates which stimulate strong healthy root action; in addition the nitrogen content assists development of stems and foliage. It is used as a dressing scattered over the surface and pricked in when preparing the ground. It has become apparent in recent years that if bonemeal is applied every year, a residue build-up of phosphate can become so high that it causes other nutrients to become locked up in the soil instead of being readily assimilated by plants; in consequence, the size of chrysanthemum blooms is reduced. A soil test should therefore be made before using bonemeal when preparing ground for chrysanthemums. Failing this, the only thing to recommend is to use it only every fourth or fifth year.

FISH MANURE

This is usually supplied as a balanced product containing other fertilizers, so the analysis varies according to the manufacturer. However, a common average analysis for fish meal is nitrogen 4·5%, phosphoric acid 9% and potash 5%. As a general fertilizer it has proved to be of great value and is one of those which can be safely used on chrysanthemum plots four to six weeks prior to planting out.

SOOT (NITROGEN 4–5%)

The use of soot unfortunately has declined considerably of late because of the advent of heating by gas, oil or electricity which has led to a scarcity of solid fuel soot and also because it is very difficult to determine if the soot has come from coal or oil-fired heating, as the latter should never be used in the garden. If soot is obtainable from household chimneys, its principal nutrient value is nitrogen. It can be used as a dressing to help lighten heavy soils but in chrysanthemum culture it excels as a deterrent to leaf-miner. Used in liquid form, by soaking a small bag of soot in water and diluting the water so that it is only just coloured, it can be sprayed over plants. Before use in this way, the soot must be stored for at least four months in a dry place exposed to the air to get rid of the sulphur.

Concentrated Mineral or Artificial Fertilizers

A considerable number of gardeners are very reluctant to use concentrated fertilizers, believing that they have a detrimental effect on the soil. It is a fact that an excessive application of this group of fertilizers will inevitably lead to a large build-up in residue values, so that fertility may be temporarily affected; but since this can also be said about the use of large quantities of farmyard manure, the inexperienced grower must learn to use all substances in moderation and have his soil tested each year as previously recommended. The following artificial fertilizers are of particular use to chrysanthemum growers.

SUPERPHOSPHATE

Although available in different concentrations, the strength most commonly marketed is 18–20% soluble phosphoric acid. Possibly one of the most popular artificials supplying phosphorus, superphosphate is manufactured by treating mineral phosphates with sulphuric acid. When mixed with sulphate of ammonia and sulphate of potash it makes a base dressing. Again, when using this commodity, the procedure of having a regular soil test should be followed rather than using superphosphate indiscriminately.

The most common analysis obtained is 18% phosphoric acid (P_2O_5) but during the Second World War a more concentrated form, known as triple superphosphate, was imported from America and is still available. This has an analysis of 48% phosphoric acid so it is essential for the grower to know exactly what strength is being used in order to obtain the right balance. The usual rate to apply the 18% analysis is 136gm per sq metre (4oz per sq yard).

NITRATE OF SODA (SODIUM NITRATE, NITROGEN 16%)

A quick-acting nitrogenous fertilizer used in chrysanthemum culture for hurrying on backward plants, this is not recommended as a base dressing, but can be of great value on light ground as it helps to bind soil particles together, thus enabling them to retain moisture more effectively. A dressing of 34gm per sq metre (1oz per sq yard) is quite sufficient if applied to the growing site before planting takes place.

SULPHATE OF AMMONIA (AMMONIUM SULPHATE, NITROGEN 21%)

This nitrogenous fertilizer made synthetically from the atmosphere has nitrogen present in the form of ammonia. Before this is suitable for absorption by plants it has to be converted to a nitrate by soil-borne bacteria and it is therefore slower acting than nitrates. This property allows it to be used as an ingredient for inclusion in base dressings, and in fact this is the best way to use the product, rather than in supplementary feeding. If however it is used as a supplementary feed it is best applied in liquid form as otherwise if the ground is dry it can have a caustic effect on the young feeding roots of plants that close to the surface. 1 teaspoonful (5ml) per $4\frac{1}{2}$ litres (1 gallon) should not cause any harm.

UREA (NITROGEN 46%)

Although technically an organic fertilizer, this is probably better considered as a concentrated artificial fertilizer because of the very high nitrogen content. Any misuse can quickly damage plants, so great care is necessary to avoid exceeding the recommended strength: 5 ml or 1 teaspoonful to $4\frac{1}{2}$ litres (1 gallon) of water will be sufficient for watering six plants grown in the open ground; used during late June and July every ten to fourteen days it helps build up good vegetative growth. It can be used as a foliar feed if nitrogen deficiency is suspected, in which case the rate of use is approximately 1gm per litre (1oz to 6 gallons). To apply this type of feed use a fine spray over plants.

NITROFORM (NITROGEN 38%)

This material provides a slow release of nitrogen in soil temperatures above 5°C (40°F) and as it does not leach from the soil it can be incorporated when digging during the winter; it will remain intact ready for release in the spring. Rate of application is 50gm per sq metre ($1\frac{1}{2}$oz per sq yard).

SULPHATE OF POTASH (POTASH 50%)

The easiest and best artificial means of supplying potash, this is generally applied at the beginning of the season when preparing ground at a handful to the sq metre (approx 1 sq yard). This slight difference in area will make no difference in its effect.

NITRATE OF POTASH (NITROGEN 14%, POTASH 46%)

This fertilizer, commonly known as saltpetre, combines both nitrogen and potassium in a form which can quickly be absorbed by plants. Here again, used as a liquid feed, it can often help backward plants. Several waterings at 1 teaspoonful (5ml) per $4\frac{1}{2}$ litres (1 gallon) of water at intervals of ten days during July and August may help backward plants produce blooms earlier.

SULPHATE OF MAGNESIUM (EPSOM SALTS, MAGNESIUM 10%)

This helps to give more intensity of colour in both flowers and foliage. It can be supplied to plants separately during June and July, but I am more in favour of using it as one of the ingredients of a base dressing applied to the growing site prior to planting out. It can also be applied with equal effect as a foliar spray at 2oz per gallon of water (50gm per 4 litres).

GENERAL BASE FERTILIZER

A very simple mixture, which supplies most of the initial nutrients required for chrysanthemum growing is 6kg (14lb) hoof and horn meal, 3kg (7lb) sulphate of ammonia, 3kg sulphate of potash and 3kg sulphate of magnesium. Applied at a handful per sq metre or sq yard and pricked into the top 15cm (6in) of the plot, it will certainly furnish plants with a good initial feed after planting out. Subsequent growth condition of plants will soon indicate if any further supplementary feeding is necessary.

Trace Elements

This is the name given to the many substances which, when applied to the soil, will help to correct its various deficiencies, with a consequent improvement in blooms. These deficiencies are often difficult to identify but are usually manifested by yellowing and chlorosis of foliage. Although trace elements are present in most seaweed-based fertilizers and indeed are also included in a number of other proprietary fertilizers, they can also be supplied by the application of various elements to the soil, mostly in minute quantities. I have found the following formula for restoring most of the trace elements to be extremely effective:

$\frac{1}{2}$kg (1lb) manganese sulphate
$\frac{1}{2}$kg (1lb) ferrous sulphate
28gm (1oz) borax
$2\frac{1}{2}$kg (5lb) bone flour

⎫ per 25 sq metres (30 sq yards) applied once every three years ⎬⎭

The bone flour is used in the role of a spreader for the other substances, otherwise extreme difficulty would be experienced in spreading these efficiently over such a wide area.

There should be no difficulty in obtaining ferrous sulphate and bone flour from any horticultural sundriesman, but borax and manganese sulphate may offer a slight problem, in which case I would suggest consulting your local chemist. Here again, borax will no doubt be kept in stock, but manganese sulphate will probably have to be ordered specially; the latter, compared with most other fertilizers, will be expensive, so if he can obtain commercial manganese sulphate rather than the highly refined product it will be very much cheaper and will serve the purpose admirably.

Having dealt with the substances which are necessary for good chrysanthemum growth, some thought must be given to formulating a manure and fertilizing programme. While this will be dealt with fully when considering the individual treatment of earlies and lates, the newcomer to chrysanthemum growing must realize from the beginning that there are no short cuts to producing good blooms. It is a fallacy to think that lack of adequate ground or compost preparation can be overcome by using fertilizers in larger quantities than those recommended. This does not mean that the fanatical approach of the exhibitor is the only formula for growing quality chrysanthemums, but rather that the amount of time available must be geared to the number of plants grown to allow sufficient time to be spent throughout the year in order to accomplish all the necessary tasks.

6 *Propagation*

Chrysanthemums can be propagated in three different ways: by division, by sowing seeds or by taking cuttings.

Division

The new grower, after wintering stools successfully, would naturally expect to divide an old plant in the same manner as with other perennials; and while this division, if practised, is suitable for ordinary purposes, a plant once flowered invariably gives maximum vigour during its first season and after this the old root system, if retained, tends to deteriorate. Production of reasonable sized blooms is best achieved from a cutting; this will give an entirely new root system, vigorous in action and able to supply the right condition for robust growth so necessary if the superior blooms that we are seeking are to be obtained.

A compromise can be reached, if desired, by using what is known as an 'Irishman's cutting'; the gardener without a greenhouse who probably grows more hardy types of chrysanthemums such as sprays and Koreans is more likely to use this type of cutting which is virtually in the form of selective division.

Once the stool produces new growths, these can be broken off as far away from the main stem as possible with small roots still attached. These shoots are then planted into either a nursery bed or seed trays, or potted individually in $7\frac{1}{2}$cm or $8\frac{3}{4}$cm pots (3in or $3\frac{1}{2}$in). While young plants produced in this manner are settling down in their new environment, protection can be given by covering them with one or two barn cloches until they are ready to be transferred to their permanent quarters in the herbaceous border.

Seeds

The sowing of seed is usually confined to the production of new cultivars where, by cross-pollination, a large quantity of seed is obtained, all of which must be flowered during its first season to find out whether any is suitable to continue being grown in succeeding years. A few specialist types such as charms and Koreans can also be raised from seed to reach full flowering size in their first season of growth. To the experimentally-minded, it is also possible to buy small quantities of seed offered for sale by nurserymen, although results range from single, spidery and spoon types to the occasional double bloom; it is very rarely indeed that a first-class cultivar is obtained in this way.

Cuttings

The vast majority of chrysanthemums are propagated in the more conventional way by taking cuttings, but certain basic equipment is needed for this operation. An unheated cold frame can be used for propagation, but as this has very strict limitations most amateurs use a slightly heated greenhouse in which a minimum temperature of 5–10°C (41–50°F) can be maintained whatever the weather. By the use of a propagator on the bench, a higher temperature can easily be maintained for propagation purposes. If the number of rooted cuttings required is comparatively small, an apple box with a sheet of glass on top will suffice; on a larger scale, rooting on the open bench is recommended, using some form of bottom heat.

SOIL HEATING

Possibly the best way of supplying bottom heat is by means of a soil-heating cable. Staging must first be covered with suitable rot-proof material—corrugated plastic sheeting is ideal for this purpose. On this the soil-heating cable is installed, embedded in a layer of sharp sand about 7½cm (3in) deep. Great care must be taken to ensure that the cable is properly covered and earthed. It cannot be overstressed that the installation of these cables should never be attempted by anyone who is not suitably qualified, because the damp conditions under which the heating cable operates do not allow even a slight margin of error. Having said this, may I also emphasize that, properly installed, there is nothing to fear. Most electricity boards will be only too pleased to advise on such installations. Once soil heating is available, it is possible to give bottom heat, which is the most efficient way to assist the rooting process of cuttings. It is a matter of choice whether a further layer of rooting medium is spread on the sharp sand for direct insertion of cuttings or if separate seed trays are used; if the latter method is practised, after inserting cuttings the seed trays are placed on the heated bench. This method has the great advantage that trays of cuttings can be readily rooted and then very easily moved to a cooler part of the house, or even removed direct into cold frames to make way for further trays. It is admitted that the heated bench is not an absolute necessity, but it is an extremely useful accessory.

ROOTING MEDIUM

Chrysanthemum cuttings will root in almost anything; indeed, there is a much-quoted story of the nurseryman who, having gathered a handful of prepared cuttings, dropped one into the dregs in the bottom of a teacup. For some reason the cup was not used again but two weeks later the cutting was noticed, complete with new roots growing. This, in fact, is not exaggeration, but it can hardly be said to be the ideal method of rooting cuttings. John Innes sterilized seed compost, peat, coarse sand, vermiculite and soil-less composts all have their devotees and are excellent media; in my own case, I have for many years used a mixture of John Innes seed compost, damp peat and Cornish grit, one third of each by bulk. While sharp sand can be used as a substitute for the Cornish grit, if it should be diffi-cult to obtain, on no account can ordinary garden soil be used, either completely or in a mixture, as this will be inviting an attack of 'damping-off'.

CONTAINERS

While some growers may still use the old system of rooting a few cuttings around the edge of small clay pots, most gardeners find that using strong wooden trays approximately 40cm × 25cm × 7½cm (16in × 10in × 3in) deep gives much better results. Trays of this size take forty-eight cuttings and are easy to stand in a propagator or on the heated bench as previously described. At least a week before they are required the trays are prepared by filling them with rooting compost. Then pressure is applied with a flat piece of wood so that the compost is firmed, leaving it at a depth of 5cm (2in). This reduc-tion from the original 7½cm (3in) gives just the right degree of firm-ness for good rooting. A layer of very fine silver or potting sand is sprinkled on the surface and, after a light watering with a fine-

rosed can, the trays can be left in the greenhouse to warm up ready
to receive cuttings.

TAKING CUTTINGS

The time for taking cuttings varies considerably according to the
different types of chrysanthemum and even here there can be a very
wide difference of acceptable dates. For example, in the large exhibition section, the cultivar 'James Bryant' needs to be rooted in
December while 'Duke of Kent' often tends to flower early and
therefore is probably best left until February before rooting.

Apart from variation in types, many other factors must be taken
into account: geographical location, height above sea level, whether
the growing site is open or protected, texture of soil and even the
individual cultural programme—all of these elements play a very
vital part. While this may not be such a tricky problem for the
average gardener, some study of timing must inevitably be undertaken, otherwise it would be quite possible for early flowering cultivars grown in the open ground not to flower before frosts commenced in the autumn, wasting much time and effort and in all
probability leading to all the blooms being spoiled.

A few notes made in a diary will soon master this aspect of chrysanthemum culture but meanwhile a detailed initial timetable will
help in solving the problem.

Assuming that all the varying types of chrysanthemums are to be
grown, a start will first be made in November when cuttings for the
very large specimen plants must be taken; an exceptionally early start
has to be made as, although the actual flowering of a mature plant
will be twelve months ahead, this long period of growth is necessary
to ensure that the number of stoppings required is obtained. This is,
however, dealt with more fully in chapter 10.

Large and medium exhibition cuttings are taken in late December
to early January, followed very closely by exhibition incurves in
January or early February. Decoratives and late singles are spread
over the period of late January to the end of February.

Growers in Australia and New Zealand who mainly cultivate late-
flowering types of chrysanthemums in the open ground will obviously
be working to a programme geared to approximately six months
later in the year because of the difference in season. In America, the
dates to take cuttings will vary considerably depending on the latitude of the grower.

Possibly the largest number of cuttings will be taken for the outdoor flowering sections and with these there are two very distinct schools of thought regarding the right time to take cuttings. The first states that cuttings should be taken during late January; then, as soon as rooted, plants are transferred to the coolest possible conditions in a cold frame. This theory, which certainly has a lot in its favour, is based on the fact that top growth will be gradual in the cool air conditions while the root system, particularly if the rooted cuttings are planted directly into the frame, will be very much larger by the time the move to their outdoor planting site becomes due. Equally emphatic are those who favour a system where cuttings are taken in early March and, because of the much higher temperatures at this time of the year, cuttings root more quickly and the plants develop very rapidly. It must be admitted that by this second method plants do not have such a large root system when they are planted out. In the hands of experienced growers, both methods can produce blooms in September of almost equal quality.

Having experimented with both systems I very much favour the first method. With the early start, rooting takes place under much more natural conditions and, because of the immediate cool treatment, produces a short-jointed plant, which is in a much more acceptable stage of development when the planned stopping date is reached. This in turn tends to give blooms in September just that much better and larger. Brought down to its simplest terms, the larger the root system when planted out, the larger resulting blooms are likely to be in September. It must be appreciated that the guiding timetable and treatment of cuttings given is for general guidance only; obviously there must be exceptions in all the varying types of chrysanthemum and the treatment of these exceptions will be mastered within one or two seasons as experience is gained.

Cuttings should, whenever possible, be taken from new basal growths in preference to those growing from the main stem; any cultivars which are shy in throwing basal cuttings will have to be propagated from stem cuttings but the growths taken should be examined carefully before use as there is a distinct chance, even at this early stage, that premature budding will take place.

After nipping off the lower leaves, a clean square cut is made through the stem with a sharp razor blade immediately below a leaf joint, or node as it is often termed. This prepared cutting will now be about 3¾cm in length (1½in) and ideally 3mm (⅛in) thick. There are growers who follow the practice of commercial tradesmen and use small tip cuttings that are about 1cm (⅜in) in length. The tradesmen are following a very carefully planned system of producing new disease-free stock in conjunction with heat treatment; small tip cuttings are an integral part of this control, and as the amateur should have more control over the stock from which he propagates, I see no real reason for such small cuttings to be necessary. The prepared cuttings are now ready for insertion into pots or boxes and my method differs from most writers in that I do not make a hole with a dibber. After immersing the cutting in a jar of weak insecticide, it is held firmly between the thumb and forefinger near its base and gently pushed into the rooting compost to a depth of about 2½cm (1in). No firming will be necessary but as soon as the tray of cuttings has been completed, an overhead watering is given with a fine-rosed can; if there are any small spaces between a cutting and the compost, the water will take some of the fine sand which was sprinkled on the surface into these spaces. The tray is now ready to place in a propagator or on the heated bench. If rooting direct into a propagating bed on the open bench is being practised, the same routine for inserting the cuttings is followed.

Using this method, good cuttings 3mm (⅛in) thick will seldom snap when being pushed into the rooting compost; if they do so, in all probability they would have been too thin to give strong well-rooted plants. It may be noted that I have not advised using a hormone rooting powder and perhaps I should hasten to emphasize that I am certainly not against the use of this aid to growth. Chrysanthemum cuttings will root quite well without assistance, so it is once more a matter of personal preference. If rooting powder is going to be used, first immerse the cutting in the jar of insecticide; then, before inserting it into the compost, the bottom 6mm (¼in) is dipped into rooting powder and the surplus shaken off. Once cuttings are finally settled in their rooting medium, subsequent watering must be administered very carefully and will depend upon the amount of natural heat from sun and the degree of bottom heat generated. Should watering become necessary, a good soaking every few days is preferable to a trickle every day. Mist propagation would avoid a considerable amount of watering but the installation of such a system hardly warrants the expense to the average gardener; it can be imitated to some extent by giving a light spraying over plants with a small pneumatic sprayer two or three times during the day and even more frequently on bright sunny days.

The time taken for rooting will vary considerably, according to conditions and amount of heat given, from ten to fourteen days in a warm greenhouse to about four or five weeks if an unheated cold frame is used. However long this rooting may take, the cuttings will indicate that a root system has been formed by the alteration in the colour of their foliage to a very much lighter colour. Some cultivars almost turn yellow at the tips when rooted, but this very soon reverts to a good healthy green colour once they are moved on.

POTTING AND BOXING ON

Once cuttings are rooted they are moved on as soon as possible. This is more urgent if rooting is taking place in peat, sand, vermiculite or any medium containing little, if any, food content; John Innes compost is able to sustain a cutting without risk of starvation for a longer period.

Whether cuttings are of late or early flowering cultivars, the initial moving on follows the same pattern. To plant them in pots, boxes or direct into a cold frame is a decision which each grower must make. Let us first consider the late cultivars and here, for convenience, a transfer into a 7½cm (3in) pot will be the natural move to make, though sometimes a slightly larger pot is necessary if the root ball is particularly strong.

Since a long period of growth is required by these late cultivars, the sooner this is done the better; sequence of potting is likely to be the same as that in which cuttings were taken, namely, large exhibition, incurves, decoratives and singles.

Removing rooted cuttings from the propagating bed or boxes is very easy if an old table fork is used. Care must be taken not to break the young root system, as a check at this stage is likely to influence the plant's whole life.

A crock is placed in the bottom of the pot and compost is added until the pot is about half full. Then carefully set the rooted cutting into position in the pot and top the remainder of the space up with more compost; give the pot a light tap on the potting bench and slightly firm the compost with your fingers. This treatment will leave a space of 1¼cm (½in) between the surface of the compost and the rim of the pot; a light watering with a fine-rosed can, and the job is completed. Subsequent moving on into larger pots is dealt with in the section on general cultivation of late-flowering types. Boxes are more convenient than pots for early-flowering cultivars, especially as the plants have only to be grown in them until planting out in the open ground. The boxes I use are the familiar tomato trays which can be obtained from almost any greengrocer without much trouble; seven of these are filled from 50kg (approx 1cwt) of compost.

There is a great temptation to overcrowd plants when setting them into trays from the propagating bench, but ample allowance must be made for the fact that these young plants make considerable growth of both foliage and roots in the weeks leading up to planting out. Twelve plants to a tray should be the maximum and in some cases, where a particular cultivar has very robust growth, nine to a tray will be necessary. The system of planting into trays is very similar to individual potting. Half fill with compost (no crocks are required), then carefully place the small plants on the compost, spreading out all the roots as far as possible without disturbing the root ball too much. Complete filling the tray with more compost and, after firming with the fingers, water with a fine-rosed can to help settle the compost around the young plants. Move into cold frames after about a week or ten days.

ASH BASE METHOD

While this method is not widely used by the general gardener it may still be of interest to learn that in recent years this system of growing on plants from the rooted cutting stage to planting out has become the practice of most top-class exhibitors of early-flowering chrysanthemums and certainly, if good exhibition plants are required, this method is highly commended. Possibly more preparatory work is involved but, to the true enthusiast, hours spent are a minor consideration if results justify the extra effort. It will be appreciated that some details vary according to the whims of individual growers but basically the sole object of this method is to produce a short-jointed plant with the largest possible root system, the ultimate of perfection for the exhibitor.

A layer of weathered ashes, about 15cm (6in) in depth, is first laid in a cold frame and on this a further layer of compost is spread to a depth of 7½cm (3in); John Innes No 2 is a suitable medium to use. A good watering is given and after about a week all will be ready to receive the rooted cuttings. These are planted into the compost with a spacing of 10cm (4in) in each direction. The object now is to encourage the roots of plants to grow through the compost and penetrate into the ashes; therefore no water is given immediately after planting, so that roots are forced to search for any moisture that is present from the preparation of the bed. Opinions differ on the point of watering. Some growers advocate watering seven to ten days after planting and subsequently when necessary; other, much stronger-willed exhibitors withhold water for two or three weeks and only lightly spray the plants on fine sunny days. Both methods appear to give similar results. For the first few days after planting the frame lights are kept closed, but after this the young plants must not be coddled and air is given on every possible occasion.

It is accepted that very sharp sand or grit can be used instead of weathered ashes as the latter are not always easy to obtain. The John Innes No 2 compost can also be replaced by the grower's own individual choice, but whatever the compost used it should be open and similar in composition to the John Innes No 2 formula.

TREATMENT OF PLANTS FROM NURSERY

Although this is not strictly propagation, all newcomers to the art of growing good chrysanthemums will, in their first growing season, take delivery of plants from a nursery, and guidance on initial treatment is essential. The same rules apply as those given for propagated cuttings regarding actual boxing or potting, but often, due to transit or possible delay in the post, some first-aid treatment may be required. Most nurserymen nowadays use a wrapping of thin polythene around plants which, if they have been well watered prior to packing, should not lose much moisture. However, if they do seem dry, any loss of moisture must first be replaced before boxing or potting can be contemplated. Plants will respond quickly if they are stood in a jar of water for several hours—overnight if necessary. Then they are set in their pots or boxes which are stood on the floor of the greenhouse for two or three days, where the conditions appertaining there will sustain the plants better than if they are immediately placed on the staging in more direct light. Once the plants recover, they can once more be moved to the cold frame and gradually given air, so that in turn these will make strong short-jointed plants in the same manner as those propagated from our own stock plants.

7 Stopping and Timing

If left to its own devices, a chrysanthemum plant, after producing one large bud on its main stem which is known as the break bud, develops into a bush-like plant bearing a multitude of small flowers. This form of growth is required for Koreans, pompons or cultivars being grown as sprays which rely on this mass presentation for effectiveness. If the intention is to grow quality flowers where single blooms on each stem are required, this exuberance must be rigidly controlled in order to achieve a size suitable for display on a show bench or in vases to enhance and beautify the home. The natural flowering time of any cultivar is seldom suitable for your requirements, whether it be to grace your garden or for the needs of an exhibitor wishing to produce blooms on a given date; timing is therefore of paramount importance to him. The keen gardener is not so worried although ultimately, since weather conditions will probably decide when the cultivar will flower, we can only try to persuade nature to abide by our actions.

Process of Stopping

The principles of stopping apply equally to both early and late-flowering cultivars; only the dates when it is practised differ. The operation itself is extremely simple and basically consists of inducing an artificial check to the plant by removing its growing tip. This causes the sap flow to be diverted into the very small embryo growths at each leaf axil and these in turn develop into stems or 'breaks' as they are usually termed; it is on these breaks that quality flowers will form. The term 'stopping' may initially confuse less experienced gardeners for, far from stopping the growth of a plant, the object of this operation is to assist it in the production of sufficient stems to furnish the required number of blooms.

NATURAL BREAK—FIRST CROWN

Many chrysanthemum catalogues advise that certain cultivars should be flowered on a natural break. This is said to occur when the plant is allowed to grow on a single stem until a bud is produced. Breaks then develop which, as with stopping, can be reduced gradually down to the number it has been decided to retain. Once these breaks are formed and begin to extend, this central or break bud is removed; if retained it would serve no useful purpose and only provide a poor bloom on a very short stem.

This natural break method is particularly useful with cultivars which tend to flower early if the conventional stopping process is applied to them. Flowers produced in this way are said to come from a natural break, first crown bud. The term 'first crown' is also used to describe the flowering buds which are obtained from a single artificial stopping.

SECOND CROWN BUDS

There are occasions when one stopping, whether by natural break or conventional stop, produces blooms much too early for your purposes and it is therefore necessary to resort to a second stopping. Although resulting blooms are invariably smaller, this decrease in size is more than compensated for by the improved form, refinement and better colour. While this system is seldom practised or indeed needed for early-flowering cultivars, in the late sections, especially exhibition incurves and singles, these additional attributes are a distinct advantage where size, although important, takes second place. The first stopping is usually made about mid-April, to be followed by the second stopping during June; no hard-and-fast rules govern the date of the second stopping, as this varies considerably according to geographical location and other conditions. Blooms obtained in this manner are said to come from second crown buds.

SECURING THE BUD

As the breaks develop, a decision has to be made regarding the number of breaks to be retained, and this will vary according to the grower's needs. The general pattern is to retain six to eight for cut-flowers or border decoration and one, two or three for exhibition

Fig. 3 Plant after a natural break:
(*a*) break buds (*b*) terminal buds.

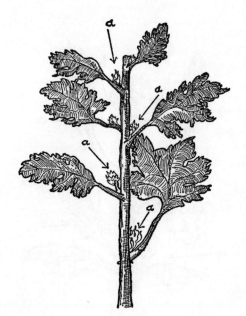

Fig. 4 Plant stopped by
removal of the growing tip
of main stem: (*a*) young
breaks forming in the leaf
axils.

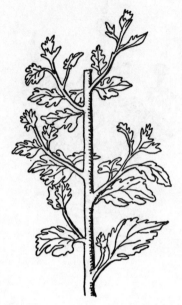

Fig. 5 'Breaks', also known as lateral growths, developing.

Fig. 6 Bud ready for 'securing': (*a*) side-shoots to be removed gradually; (*b*) re-move small buds around main central bud when large enough to handle.

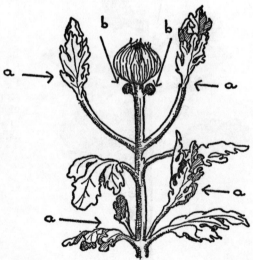

Fig. 7 Plant fully disbudded with six lateral growths fully developed, and the first crown bud secured.

Fig. 8 Plant after two stoppings: (*a*) first stop, (*b*) second stop. The drawing is not to scale so the stem, after the second stop, will be longer than it appears.

earlies and lates, apart from singles where more are retained according to the strength of the plant. It is more than likely that few breaks, if any, will have to be removed in plants wanted purely for garden decoration, but in the realms of exhibition, restriction is very necessary. The type of plant, whether an early or late-flowering cultivar and its soil or potting conditions have great bearing on this important facet of chrysanthemum culture, but are better dealt with individually in the appropriate chapter. However, the action leading to and affecting the securing of the bud is the same in all cases.

During June, July and August, breaks retained will in turn form side-shoots from each leaf axil, and these are removed when large enough to handle without risk of damaging the main stem. Possibly the best method is to nip these out, leaving a small stump still on the main stem; otherwise, should the outer skin of the plant's main stem be damaged accidentally, when this skin tightens in the healing process it can cause the stem to lean over slightly—and, while this will possibly not be noticed in garden decoration, a bent stem is considered to be a fault on the show bench.

By late July or early August in the case of early-flowering cultivars and August to early September for the late-flowering sections, a main flower bud forms at the tip of each break which in turn is surrounded by a cluster of other small buds or side-shoots. These again are allowed to develop until large enough to be removed safely, one at a time, over a period of seven to fourteen days; the temptation to prod around and remove these buds or shoots with a penknife while they are very small is one that must be avoided at all costs, for there is far too great a risk that this will lead to a damaged stem.

The time which elapses from 'securing the bud' until harvesting a mature bloom varies from six to twelve weeks depending on the cultivar, type of bloom and weather conditions. As a guide, many early-flowering medium cultivars take six to seven weeks while some large exhibition blooms, regarded by many as the prima donnas of the chrysanthemum world, take as long as twelve weeks to reach full maturity; but the various time periods will be assimilated as experience is gained.

RUNNING-ON

It is very unlikely that any gardeners other than exhibitors will need to use the system of running-on but it is an integral part of chrysanthemum-growing knowledge and I would be failing in my duty to keen gardeners if I did not explain this fully. In spite of elaborate actions which are taken to produce blooms by a given date, nature sometimes decides to demonstrate that she alone is still responsible and in consequence main flowering buds on certain cultivars develop far too early for show purposes. Although resulting blooms will be smaller, it is possible to delay a plant's flowering by as much as two or three weeks. When the main bud forms, this is pinched out and one of the surrounding side-shoots is allowed to grow on in its place. This in turn forms a bud and is then secured as already described. The principle here is that it is better to have a smaller bloom which can be usefully employed or exhibited rather than an earlier larger bloom which would be useless. To an exhibitor, every bloom which cannot be shown is considered to be a waste—he seldom uses it as a cut-flower for decoration in the home, but normally leaves it on the plant, 'just in case'. This is the main difference between the enthusiastic gardener and the dedicated exhibitior.

TREATMENT OF LARGE EXHIBITION CULTIVARS

Large exhibition cultivars are purely exhibition blooms, as the name implies. Best blooms are obtained early in November and timing must be arranged with this in mind. Since stopping dates vary widely in this section, both with the cultivar and its geographical position, it would be very foolish to try and detail exact dates. A vital part of successful growing, therefore, is to keep records, which after one or two seasons will furnish an acceptable average date if taken in conjunction with weather conditions—long-range weather forecasting is just another subject that somehow has to be mastered in pursuit of this absorbing hobby of growing good chrysanthemums.

The tables at the end of this chapter are intended purely as a guide. The dates given have proved to be average amongst many well-known gardeners, mostly growing blooms in the south of England, to whom I am indebted for their assistance. An adjustment of seven to fourteen days should, in most cases, suit gardeners further north.

Maximum size, so vital to this kind of bloom, will only be obtained if plants are restricted to one bloom. Breaks obtained from the original stop require gradual restriction until two are left, the final reduction down to one break being made when these are approximately 60–75cm (2–2½ft) in length.

TREATMENT OF MEDIUM EXHIBITION CULTIVARS

Medium exhibition blooms are smaller versions of the large exhibition section. They are usually flowered on first crown buds from a natural break or a stop given during late April or early May.

They should carry a crop of flowers dependent on the strength and vigour of the plant. Three blooms per plant for exhibition and six to eight for other purposes are the usual numbers these will sustain.

TREATMENT OF EXHIBITION INCURVES

The attractiveness of incurves relies completely on their almost perfect globular form and in this respect they are without doubt the nearest to perfection that can be asked of any type of chrysanthemum. It is not surprising that they are looked upon by many admirers as the aristocrats of the family.

To obtain this form, many cultivars in the section require blooms to be flowered on second crown buds from a first stop given during April followed by a second one in June. Obviously there must be exceptions to the rule and here guidance given in nurserymen's catalogues will prove invaluable. It may well be, however, that while this information will provide a bloom on time, the perfect end-product which is so sought after will materialize only from much experimentation.

Selecting which breaks to retain must be done with great care, as there is always a leaning towards an inherent weakness in the stems of incurves; three or four blooms are advised for these plants. The breaks chosen should be as robust as possible and any which do not reach these very stringent standards are best removed in the early stages, with the proviso that three at least be retained, otherwise blooms will tend to be coarse and have poor form.

TREATMENT OF DECORATIVES

Chrysanthemums in the decorative sections, both reflexed and intermediate, although extensively grown for exhibition purposes, are possibly grown more by non-exhibitors than any other of the late-flowering sections as they make ideal plants for housing in September to provide blooms during winter months. For November shows most cultivars respond to first crown buds from a natural break; if the

I   Gypsy. Early flowering medium chrysanthemum (NCS Classification 24B).

break bud has not arrived by mid-June, plants should be artificially stopped.

There is also a fascination in producing blooms from your own greenhouse around Christmas time, and this is possible with a certain element of luck. It must be stressed that all timing is very dependent upon many other factors, weather and temperature being two of them. During October and November, a sunny day soon sends greenhouse temperatures rocketing. Certain cultivars such as 'Balcombe Perfection' and 'Fred Shoesmith' are ideal for Christmas flowering if they are stopped in mid-April and again in late July and it is suggested that six breaks should be grown for this purpose.

TREATMENT OF ANEMONE-CENTRED AND SINGLE CULTIVARS

With very few exceptions, best results are obtained from two stoppings, the first in mid-April, the second in mid-June. These two types of chrysanthemum are very free-flowering so need severe restriction in the number of breaks in order to obtain any quality in the bloom. The strength of growth of each individual plant must be taken into account, but generally six breaks are retained after the second stopping for large singles and nine for mediums and anemone-centred cultivars.

TREATMENT OF EARLY-FLOWERING CULTIVARS

The largest group of chrysanthemums are the outdoor flowering types and although they have various forms, similar to late greenhouse cultivars, they can be taken as one for timing and stopping. Almost without exception they are grown on first crown buds and break far more freely than the late-flowering plants.

The time of stopping extends over a long period from April to early June. Apart from cultivars which, if not stopped in April or early May, would flower too late for the shows or before frost damage, there are many which will break naturally by early June without an artificial stopping.

Plants grown in borders and beds for garden decoration can be stopped twice to encourage more breaks. On the other hand, if a natural break has not already taken place, a stop given at the end of May after which the plant is allowed to grow on without any disbudding is another method employed in borders. There are many lovely kinds of chrysanthemums which come into this category, Koreans, pompons and sprays being the chief representatives.

HEIGHT OF PLANTS

Stopping, along with other factors, has a direct effect on the final height of plants. When two stoppings are given, stems will grow 45–61cm (18in to 2ft) taller than if a natural break or one stopping is given. In the late-flowering groups, singles and some large exhibition cultivars are the chief offenders against height, and heights of 2 metres (6½ft) are not uncommon.

Stopping and Timing Tables

No advice on this involved subject would be complete without detailing the main factors which influence the correct timing of blooms for show purposes. These are mainly the time when cuttings are taken and the stopping dates given in the following tables. It must be emphasized that all dates are only intended as a guideline to the less experienced until such time as they have a more accurate date to conform with their particular local conditions. The non-exhibitor will not be unduly concerned with accurate timing, so dates given here will be quite sufficient.

LATE-FLOWERING (INDOOR) CULTIVARS
Large Exhibition

NB = natural break; all NB cultivars which have not made a break by end of May should be stopped

Cultivar	Colour	Date cuttings rooted	Stopping dates
Albert Shoesmith	Y	Early January	10 May
Charles Shoesmith	LB	Mid January	NB
Cream Duke	PY	Early January	10 May
Duke of Kent	W	Early January	10 May
George Edwards	PP	Late December	NB
Gigantic	S	Early January	15 May
Harry Gee	PP	Early January	20 May
James Bryant	R	Early December	7 March
Jessie Habgood	W	Early January	7 May
Keith Luxford	P	Early December	20 February
Leviathan	O	Early January	15 April & 30 May
Lilac Prince	P	Early January	15 May

Cultivar	Colour	Date cuttings rooted	Stopping dates
Mark Woolman	Y	Late December	25 April
Shirley Champion	Y	Early January	15 April
Shirley Primrose	Y	Early January	15 March & NB
Silver Gigantic	O	Early January	15 May
Woking Rose	P	Mid January	5 April & 5 June
Yellow Duke of Kent	Y	Early January	10 May

Medium Exhibition

All NB cultivars which have not made a break by end of May should be stopped

Cultivar	Colour	Date cuttings rooted	Stopping dates
Amethyst	Pu	Mid January	1 May
Connie Mayhew	Y	Mid January	20 May
Cossack	R	Mid December	1 March & 15 May
Lundy	W	Early January	10 May
Majestic	LB	Late December	5 May
Red Majestic	R	Late December	5 May
Surrey White	W	Early January	NB
Tropical Lady	P	Early January	15 May
Winn Quinn	Y	Early January	NB

Exhibition Incurved

All NB cultivars which have not made a break by end of May should be stopped

LARGE-FLOWERED

Cultivar	Colour	Date cuttings rooted	Stopping dates
Audrey Shoesmith	P	Late December	15 April & 7 June
Eva Randall	LB	Mid February	10 June
Mavis Shoesmith	P	Mid February	NB
Polar Gem	W	Mid January	15 April & 10 June
Red Shirley Model	O	Mid January	15 May
Shirley Model	P	Mid January	15 May
Welcome News	LB	Early February	NB
Woolman's Perfecta	W	Early February	NB
Woolman's Royal	P	Early February	NB
Yellow Marvel	Y	Mid January	15 April & 10 June

Cultivar	Colour	Date cuttings rooted	Stopping dates
MEDIUM-FLOWERED			
Brett Williams	Y	Mid January	10 June
Dorothy Foley	P	Mid January	12 June
Maylen	W	Late February	20 June
Minstrel Boy	LB	Mid February	NB
Ron Shoesmith	W	Early February	NB
Vera Woolman	Y	Early February	NB
Waterloo	B	Mid February	10 June

Reflexed Decoratives

All NB cultivars which have not make a break by 15 June should be stopped

LARGE-FLOWERED			
Bridal Gown	W	Early January	15 April & 15 June
Crimson Lake	R	Mid January	NB
Elizabeth Woolman	P	Early February	10 June
Jim Draycott	W	Mid February	12 June
Mary Selvey	O	Mid January	1 June
Mona Davis	P	Mid January	25 May
Ron James	Y	Early January	5 May
Walker's Jewel	PP	Early February	7 June
MEDIUM-FLOWERED			
Capri	Pu	Late January	NB
Golden Princess Anne	Y	Late February	20 June
Joy Hughes	P	Mid January	NB
My Lady	P	Mid January	20 May
Penguin	W	Mid February	Mid June
Princess Anne	P	Late February	20 June
Regency	Pu	Early February	15 June
Shirley Garnet	R	Early February	7 June
Stuart Shoesmith	LB	Late February	25 June
Woking Scarlet	R	Early February	NB

Intermediate Decoratives

All NB cultivars which have not made a break by 15 June should be stopped

LARGE-FLOWERED			
Balcombe Perfection	B	Early January	25 May
Beacon	R	Mid January	30 May

Cultivar	Colour	Date cuttings rooted	Stopping dates
Cora Till	W	Mid January	7 June
Crimson Daily Mirror	O	Mid January	15 April & 15 June
Daily Mirror	Pu	Mid January	15 April & 15 June
Diplomat	W	Early February	15 June
Fair Lady	P	Early February	15 June
Fred Shoesmith	W	Mid January	25 May
Golden Gown	Y	Late January	NB
Gold Foil	Y	Mid January	10 April & 15 June
Harmony	LB	Mid January	NB
Olympic Queen	P	Early February	15 June
Orange Fair Lady	LB	Early February	15 June
Purple Glow	Pu	Mid January	12 April & 5 June
Silver Haze	P	Early February	NB

MEDIUM-FLOWERED

Bill Holbrook	W	Early February	7 June
Brenda Till	PY	Early February	NB
Jack Wilmot	Y	Early February	NB
Leslie Tandy	Pu	Early February	7 June
New Era	Pu	Early February	NB
Woking Perfection	R	Early February	NB

Anemones

Long Island Beauty	W	Early February	14 April & 14 June
Marion Stacey	Pu	Early February	14 April & 14 June
Raymond Mouncey	R	Early February	14 April & 14 June
Rolinda	LB	Early February	14 April & 14 June
Thora	P	Early February	14 April & 14 June

Singles

LARGE-FLOWERED

Albert Cooper	Y	Early February	14 April & 14 June

Cultivar	Colour	Date cuttings rooted	Stopping dates
Audax	P	Early February	14 April & 14 June
Anina	Y	Early February	14 April & 14 June
Broadacre	W	Early February	14 April & 14 June
Cleone	PP	Early February	14 April & 14 June
Crimson Crown	R	Early February	14 April & 14 June
Midlander	B	Early February	14 April & 14 June
Peggy Stevens	Y	Early February	14 April & 14 June
Peter Robinson	Y	Late January	15 March & 25 April
Preference	P	Early February	14 April & 14 June
Uranus	R	Early February	14 April & 14 June
Woolman's Glory	B	Early February	14 April & 14 June
MEDIUM-FLOWERED			
Alice Fitton	Pu	Early February	14 April & 14 June
Alliance	B	Early February	14 April & 14 June
Chesswood Beauty	R	Early February	14 April & 14 June
Edwin Painter	Y	Early February	14 April & 14 June
Jinx	W	Early February	14 April & 14 June
Lilian Jackson	P	Early February	14 April & 14 June
Mason's Bronze	B	Early February	14 April & 14 June
Nancy Sherwood	Y	Early February	14 April & 14 June
Radiant	B	Early February	14 April & 14 June

Cultivar	Colour	Date cuttings rooted	Stopping dates
Stargazer	Y	Early February	14 April & 14 June
Sunsilk	LB	Early February	14 April & 14 June

Sprays

Late-flowering sprays (including American sprays) are too numerous to list. They are best rooted as late cuttings during late April and early May and stopped mid-July

Spidery

Rayonnante (there are many colour sports of this cultivar)	P	Mid February	7 June

OCTOBER FLOWERING CULTIVARS

These are grown in open ground as earlies or in pots as lates; the times given are for normal flowering—adjustments will need to be made to obtain flowering outside the normal October season.

Incurved Decoratives

Cheddar	Y	Mid February	NB
Joan Livermore	Y	Mid February	20 May

Reflexed Decoratives

John Riley	R	Mid January	15 April
Margaret Billett	Pu	Mid February	7 May
White May	W	Mid February	NB

Intermediate Decoratives

Amy Shoesmith	P	Early February	25 April
Gold Plate	Y	Early February	10 May

EARLY FLOWERING (OUTDOOR) CULTIVARS

All NB cultivars which have not made a break by early June should be stopped

Incurved Decoratives

LARGE-FLOWERED

Ermine	W	Early March	20 May
Ernest Avison	W	Mid February	25 May

Cultivar	Colour	Date cuttings rooted	Stopping dates
Joyce Gurr	W	Mid February	25 May
Margaret Riley	P	Late February	1 June
Pat Amos	W	Mid February	20 May
White Margaret Riley	W	Late February	1 June
Yellow Pat Amos	PY	Mid February	20 May
MEDIUM-FLOWERED			
Hilton	W	Mid February	25 May
Iris Riley	P	Mid February	20 May
Marjorie Boden	Y	Mid February	20 May
Martin Riley	Y	Late February	NB
Nancy Matthews	W	Late February	NB
Skipper	LB	Late February	25 May
Yellow Nuggett	Y	Mid February	25 May

Reflexed Decoratives

Cultivar	Colour	Date cuttings rooted	Stopping dates
LARGE-FLOWERED			
Alpine Snow	W	Mid February	15 May
Ambition	Y	Mid February	25 May
Brian Russon	Y	Mid February	15 May
Bruera	W	Late February	30 May
Camito	W	Mid February	15 May
Cecely Starmer	P	Late February	25 May
Cherry Tracy Waller	R	Mid February	20 May
Grace Riley	B	Mid February	25 May
Grandstand	B	Mid February	15 May
Lona May	Y	Mid February	10 May
Parasol	P	Late February	1 June
Salmon Tracy Waller	S	Mid February	20 May
Smart Fella	Y	Mid January	10 April
Tom Briggs	W	Late January	7 May
Tracy Waller	P	Mid February	20 May
MEDIUM-FLOWERED			
Alice Jones	LB	Mid February	15 May
Barry Wiggins	LB	Late February	NB
Bellair	Pu	Late February	NB
Broadway	Pu	Late February	20 May
Bronze Eve Gray	B	Mid February	7 June
Early Red Cloak	R	Late February	7 June
Eve Gray	P	Mid February	7 June
Fenny	PP	Mid February	30 May
Harry Scovell	LB	Mid February	25 May

Cultivar	Colour	Date cuttings rooted	Stopping dates
Karen Rowe	P	Mid February	25 May
Leprechaun	P	Late February	25 May
Mexico	R	Late February	7 June
Munich	Pu	Mid February	5 June
New Stylist	Y	Mid February	25 May
Pamela Thompson	W	Late February	NB
Redhead	R	Late February	25 May
Rosa Pugh	Pu	Late February	25 May
Pretty Polly	Pu	Mid February	20 May
Sonny Riley	Y	Late February	25 May
Value	LB	Early January	15 April
Woolley Crimson	R	Late February	20 May
Woolley Dandy	R	Early February	20 April
Yellow Value	Y	Early January	15 April
Yvonne Arnaud	P	Late February	10 June

Intermediate Decoratives

LARGE-FLOWERED

Cultivar	Colour	Date cuttings rooted	Stopping dates
Alec Bedser	PY	Late February	10 June
Christine Hall	PP	Mid February	20 May
Crown of Gold	Y	Late February	1 June
Ethel Edmonds	PY	Mid February	25 May
Evelyn Bush	W	Mid February	25 May
Explosion	Y	Early February	10 May
Flo Cooper	Y	Mid February	7 May
Frances Margerison	W	Early February	15 May
Gladys Sharpe	Y	Late January	7 May
Goldington Queen	W	Late February	1 June
Keystone	Pu	Mid February	25 May
Pink Goldington Queen	P	Late February	1 June
Red Keystone	R	Mid February	25 May
Rosedew	P	Mid February	25 May
Shirley Victoria	LB	Mid February	20 May
Soccer	Y	Early February	15 May
White Christine Hall	W	Mid February	20 May
Yes Sir	W	Mid February	15 May
Yellow Ethel Edmonds	Y	Mid February	25 May

MEDIUM-FLOWERED

Cultivar	Colour	Date cuttings rooted	Stopping dates
Alistair Doig	LB	Late February	15 May
Bill Else	Y	Late February	25 May
Bonigold	Y	Mid February	25 May

Cultivar	Colour	Date cuttings rooted	Stopping dates
Bronze People		Mid February	1 June
Cricket	W	Mid February	1 June
Dairy Cream	Y	Mid February	25 May
George Hughes	Y	Mid February	25 May
Golden Market	LB	Mid February	30 May
Honeywell	Y	Mid February	25 May
Lyngford	P	Mid February	5 June
Mariette	PP	Mid February	15 May
Parakeet	Pu	Late February	25 May
Pendower	W	Mid February	15 May
Primrose Cricket	PY	Mid February	1 June
Sombrero	Y	Mid February	10 May
Stephen Bowdidge	Y	Late February	5 June
Tibshelf Gem	Y	Mid February	5 June
Topper	LB	Late February	25 May
Yellow Cricket	Y	Mid February	1 June

Anemones

Catena	B	Late February	15 June
Premiere	Y	Late February	15 June

Singles

Kitty	P	Late February	NB

Pompons (*True and Semi-pompons*)

No disbudding after initial stopping or NB

Andy Pandy	Y	Early March	NB
Brighteye	Y	Early March	NB
Bronze Fairie	B	Early March	NB
Cameo	W	Early March	NB
Denise	Y	Early March	NB
Fairie	P	Early March	NB
Poppet	Y	Early March	NB
Solly	Y	Early March	NB
Whimsy	Pu	Early March	NB

Sprays

No disbudding after initial stopping or NB

Adelaine	W	Early March	NB
Agata	LB	Early March	NB

Cultivar	Colour	Date cuttings rooted	Stopping dates
Anna Marie	W	Early March	NB
Aurora Queen	R	Early March	NB
Clarette Queen	W	Early March	NB
Claudia Queen	B	Early March	NB
Dusky	R	Early March	NB
Gerrie Hoek	P	Early March	NB
Gertrude	P	Early March	NB
Golden Orfe	Y	Early March	NB
Lilian Hoek	B	Early March	NB
Lucida	Y	Early March	NB
Madelaine	P	Early March	NB
Nathalie	Pu	Early March	NB
Patricia	R	Early March	NB
Piccolo	PY	Early March	NB
Pinocchio	LB	Early March	NB
Pennine Cream	PY	Early March	NB
Pennine Orange	B	Early March	NB
Pennine Pink	P	Early March	NB
Pennine Purple	Pu	Early March	NB
Pennine Red	B	Early March	NB
Pennine Shell	S	Early March	NB
Pennine Yellow	Y	Early March	NB
Purple gem	Pu	Early March	NB

There is a very large range of cultivars in many colours prefixed by the title 'Pennine'; those listed above are a few examples.

SPRAYS WITH SINGLE BLOOMS

Bronze Elite	B	Early March	NB
Dark Elite	Pu	Early March	NB
Pink Elite	P	Early March	NB
Red Elite	R	Early March	NB
Salmon Pye	P	Early March	NB

8 *Cultivation of Early-Flowering Chrysanthemums*

Chrysanthemums cannot be accused of being faddy plants as they always strive to produce good blooms irrespective of the type of soil, their planting position or even general environment. However, in spite of this willingness to please, there is a great deal of human assistance which can be given to nature and in return vastly improved growth can be expected resulting in blooms of such excellence that anyone who openly expresses objections to gardening must be forced to admit that the production of such blooms is worthwhile.

To obtain this perfection it is necessary to 'pay attention to detail', one of the first rules impressed upon me by an expert grower more years ago than I care to remember. His second rule, though simple enough, contains a wealth of advice in a few words: 'doing the right thing at the right time'.

The first attempt at putting these rules into practice is concerned with choice of planting position. More often than not we have little control of site or aspect, as most gardeners become house-owners first and, in the course of time, gardeners, keen or otherwise. The most open part of the garden possible should be chosen, where there are no over-hanging trees, buildings or fences; if there is room for a special bed to be set aside for chrysanthemums, the first step on the road to success is definitely assured. There may be some gardeners who wish only to cultivate plants in mixed borders but basic principles affecting preparation of ground will still apply, ensuring as far as possible there is no disturbance to permanent residents in the border. It would be unwise to start with a large number of plants until the amount of work involved is known, so I would suggest between fifty and a hundred plants in an open bed for exhibition or cut-flowers, plus a few plants of sprays, poms and Koreans in a border for general garden decoration.

A plot measuring 4 metres by 3 metres (approx 12ft by 10ft) will accommodate fifty plants without any overcrowding and certainly will not demand too much time for preparing and maintaining it in good heart.

Digging

This has to be carried out by most of us at weekends during the autumn and winter, but whenever possible, if heavy soil can be dug well before Christmas to allow frosts to assist in the breaking-down process, it will make a world of difference. Light soils will benefit by being left until February or early March as the finer particles which make up the soil tend to consolidate more quickly. Double digging is not necessary as a matter of routine, but will greatly assist in bringing heavy ground into good condition. Additionally, if a plot has been worked for several years, there is a distinct tendency for a hard layer to form just below the surface at approximately one spit deep; and if left undisturbed, this solid layer leads to bad drainage and will set up sour soil conditions quite unattractive to the root system of any plant.

It has often been said, by many experts, that to dig without incorporating something is a complete waste of time. While it must be admitted that the application of farmyard manure every second year will not necessarily keep on improving the soil, used in reasonable quantities there is probably nothing else which will assist more in the production of good chrysanthemums. If a 9-litre (2-gallon) bucket of farmyard manure or its substitute is incorporated into the top spit as digging proceeds, this should be quite adequate for retaining sufficient humus in the soil to enable other fertilizers to be given the chance of functioning correctly. Many town-dwellers find that a supply of good farmyard manure is almost unobtainable. In such cases the use of well-moistened peat in conjunction with a general fertilizer is recommended. Any proprietary chrysanthemum fertilizer can be used at the rate of a handful per sq metre (sq yard). On the other hand, a balanced fish manure fertilizer is exceptionally good for this purpose, particularly as it consists mostly of slower-acting organics.

During April, final preparation of the ground ready for planting out can be made. This must be completed when the ground is not too wet; consequently it is necessary to wait for ideal conditions. Treading around on wet ground, particularly if your soil is heavy, will ensure the undoing of all the attempted improvements in the soil structure you have worked so hard to effect by digging and aerating during winter months. Only the top 7½–10cm (3–4in) of soil needs to be pricked over, making sure you break down any lumps which may still remain; then, either using the fork or by raking, leave a nice tilth to the plot so that it will settle down slightly by the time planting is commenced.

It is as well at this stage if a dressing of fertilizer with a higher nitrogen content is incorporated in the final surface preparation, thus allowing sufficient time for chemical reaction to make it readily available for plants after setting out. In chapter 5, advice was given on various fertilizers and while it will eventually be a matter of personal preference as to which is used, I can vouch for 50m (1½–2oz) of nitroform combined with a dressing of 25gm (1oz) sulphate of magnesium per sq metre (sq yard) at this stage. Ultimately, by experimentation, it will be found which manures and fertilizers suit particular conditions; it is therefore of paramount importance that, from the outset, records are kept for reference purposes. It is easy to know what is being done at the present time, but it is an entirely different matter a few months later to try remembering how much of a particular fertilizer was applied and the exact date and stage of application.

While final soil preparation is continuing, care must be taken not to neglect plants still in the cold frames. Hardening-off should continue at all times and, as the middle of April approaches, it should be possible to leave lights off completely during the day, only replacing them at night if frost threatens. By early May, lights can be left off as the time for planting out approaches. It cannot be emphasized too strongly that, although the plants are still in frames, when lights are open or completely off protection from the first attentions of birds must be given; otherwise the little devils will soon be amongst the plants or perching on the edge of the frames calmly nipping out all the growing tips. Although adding considerable enjoyment to their diet, this will completely upset any attempts at timing blooms. If a few canes are pushed into the ground around the outside of the frame, black tacking cotton can then be wound round the canes which, although it is the oldest method, I find still to be the best. May I, however, appeal to all gardeners, on no account to use nylon or anything else that will not readily snap if a bird flies into it; otherwise it may become terribly tangled up in it and perhaps maimed.

Planting

Possibly the greatest mistake made by many beginners is to plant out much too early; while the actual time is dependent upon weather and geographical position, danger often lies in the fact that an early period of good weather may encourage a grower's enthusiasm to launch into great activity and start planting out, only to have a disastrous late spell of heavy frosts come along; while plants may not actually be killed by this they can suffer such a severe check at this young stage that it will be reflected throughout their lives. In most years the middle to end of May provides much better conditions weatherwise than will be experienced during April, but naturally, while awaiting the best possible conditions, there is no need to waste precious time as final preparation of the planting site can be carried out. In mixed perennial borders, where small areas sufficient to take six to nine plants are allocated, there is little in the way of further preparation required but in special beds canes or stakes should be set out in the final planting positions. Bamboo canes are much favoured by most gardeners and initially one stout cane $1\frac{1}{4}$ metres (4ft) in length is inserted in the ground. If planting in double rows, it is necessary to allow a distance of 40cm (15in) in each direction between plants, with a pathway 75cm ($2\frac{1}{2}$ft) wide between each pair of rows. It is possible that greater use of the area available is required, in which case planting can be done in rows of three instead of two with the same pathway distance between. When pushing canes into the ground, nasty eye injuries can be avoided if simple precautions are taken. Never stand directly over the top of a cane, for if it snaps, as so often happens with the bottom part of older canes, in all probability you will fall on to it with a great risk of severely injuring an eye. It is far better to take up a squatting position before you push the cane into the ground, so that if it snaps, while you may fall forward, it is unlikely that any injury will be sustained, except perhaps to dignity. On a reasonably large scale, plants can be supported in a similar manner to that employed by commercial growers where plastic-covered mesh about 25cm (9in) square is laid on the ground, covering the length of the bedding-out area. Plants can then be set in the spaces and as they grow the mesh is gradually raised, supported at intervals with strong wooden stakes. Growth is not held rigid and plants can move slightly with the wind, avoiding any damage. This system is an easy way of supporting plants, avoiding the laborious task of individual tying every 15–25cm (6–9in) as stems develop.

When suitable weather conditions allow planting to commence, the job is simplicity itself. Just make a hole with a trowel as near to the cane as possible, a little wider and deeper than the ball of roots will be. Carefully remove the plant from its box or pot, which should have been well watered the previous evening, place it in the hole and, after drawing surrounding soil around the plant, firm it in with fingers and knuckles leaving a small depression around the stem to encourage rainfall to circulate around the roots. Tie the plant loosely to the cane, sprinkle a few slug pellets around and label with the name of the cultivar. Once more immediate protection with black cotton against the ravages of birds must be taken, in the same manner as when the plants were in frames—but our protection programme cannot end there. Indeed it appears as if the gods are watching us, almost as soon as planting is completed, inevitably strong gale-force winds start to blow and young plants often become defoliated. While they will survive, to lose their leaves at this stage causes a severe check at a time when every bit of energy should be used for their establishment in new soil. If some protection can be given on the prevailing windward side by using hessian, polythene sheeting or any other available material, leaves will soon begin to toughen up so that after about two weeks they will be much more resistant to the elements. In the absence of anything else, it is surprising how much protection can be obtained by pushing a few twiggy branches into the ground.

Watering

Once plants are set out in the open ground, the question of watering must be considered. If a reasonable amount of rainfall could be guaranteed at regular intervals, there would be no problem. Nature, unfortunately, is not so obliging; nevertheless, any watering programme must be administered with a due allowance for rain. It has been generally accepted over the years that immediately after planting, young roots should be encouraged to forage for any available moisture, thereby establishing the plant much more quickly. While this may be correct to a degree, I have never been able to accept the advice not to water at all, even if plants flag; it does not seem logical that continual flagging over a period of a week or ten days will not have some detrimental effects on the plants. Common sense must dictate our actions, so that, rightly or wrongly, my initial action is to water plants in immediately after planting, so helping soil settle around the roots. After this, great discretion is used depending upon rainfall and amount of sun, but, possibly because, like most men, I am still a boy at heart and enjoy doing it, I hose the plot over during

II   Show stand by Alan Wren Nurseries.

the evening after two or three days of drying weather from the time of planting until early June.

During the rest of the growing season, when watering is necessary, giving small amounts every two or three days does more harm than good. A good soaking once a week will be far more effective, but how do we measure a good soaking? Again, opinions vary, but I endeavour to ensure that each plant receives at least $4\frac{1}{2}$ litres (1 gallon) of water by means of a irrigation hose which can be left in position for a length of time which has been previously calculated from the rate of flow of the main water supply. It should perhaps be explained that all my chrysanthemum growing has been carried out on very light soil; obviously watering will be less frequent on the heavier, more retentive type of soil.

Mulching

Often through lack of time or restrictions on the use of artificial watering, alternative methods of retaining necessary moisture have to be practised and, if applied correctly, the art of mulching cannot be bettered. The first accepted method is to cover the ground with organic matter $7\frac{1}{2}$cm (3in) deep. Well-rotted manure, if obtainable, is possibly best for this purpose, but often scarcity demands the use of a suitable substitute. Probably the most widely used material is moist peat, which has the additional benefit of being comparatively cheap; if hop manure is added to this at the rate of 1 part hop manure to 8 parts of peat, as with manure, it will also help feed the very fine surface roots which penetrate into the mulch. It is essential to water the soil thoroughly before any mulch is applied; unless this is done, it will take a very long time for rain or any watering to penetrate through the mulching layer into the soil and plants in the interim period may suffer a severe check through lack of water, although the surface will appear to be thoroughly wet. Of course there are many other materials which can be used for mulching: composted straw, garden compost or any medium which has been thoroughly rotted. There is, however, one further means of conserving moisture if manure or its substitute is not available, which can be classed under the heading of mulching. Originally introduced commercially, this method has been used successfully by a number of top-class amateurs and simply consists of placing a length of 1,000-gauge black polythene on the ground and cutting holes $12\frac{1}{2}$cm (5in) in diameter at planting positions. Plants are then set in these holes in the same manner as ordinary planting. This sheet of polythene is left in position throughout the season. It stifles the growth of weeds and, while holding moisture does not prevent rainfall from seeping in at the sides or through the planting holes.

Feeding

Many gardeners are misled into believing chrysanthemums are such gross feeders that to obtain the size and quality demanded by present-day standards, all that is necessary is to apply large amounts of fertilizers during the actual growing season. Nothing could be farther from the truth: if the ground is not properly prepared before planting, no amount of added fertilizers can overcome this lack of preparation. However, with humus present in soil, aeration during the winter and general conditioning, all is ready for the successful use of supplementary feeding.

At one time, feeding outdoor chrysanthemums in growth was governed by one all-important factor: the use of higher nitrogen feeds up until buds were secured and then, after a short period of rest, a switch to a higher potash feed; all feeding stopped as soon as the slightest trace of colour was visible. With increased research, possibly more knowledge has been gained but, more important, many gardeners with inquiring minds have not been content to sit back and accept this old teaching. As a result of experiments, entirely new concepts in feeding have been evolved. I do not ask you to accept these without trial but certainly, with study, the general principle can be adapted to suit all conditions.

Basically, if a plant can be grown from planting out with stems in a reasonably ripe condition, higher nitrogen feeds can be used until a much later date than was previously thought. It may well be asked, why bother with the slightly higher risk of possible damping of blooms as they mature, which must always be present in any form of nitrogen feeding? The simple answer is that if each fully developed floret can be coaxed into growing 5–6cm ($\frac{1}{4}$in) longer, with the build-up in layers of florets, a mature bloom must in consequence be larger, certainly large enough in most cases to beat opposition from blooms grown with the older and more conventional feeding programme.

How, then, is this type of feeding put into operation? The discussion on fertilizers in chapter 5 left open a very wide choice, but a start must be made somewhere, and so the following programme is intended as a guide only. It is suggested that a trial first be made of a fixed number of control plants, careful notes being taken of the analysis of feed given and time applied. I would recommend the use of nitroform in preparation of the ground because of its properties of slowly releasing nitrogen over a long period, although its very high nitrogen content, usually 38 per cent, is not all taken up at once—indeed this amount would probably be enough to blow the plant out of the ground if it were. The rest of the programme must now be conditioned to type of weather and the development of plants, remembering that we do not want lush plants at any stage, but rather balanced growth; slightly riper wood is to be preferred. Whether to use dry or liquid fertilizers is once more a matter of choice and common sense. More liquid feed will probably be used in a dry season and, conversely, dry feed scattered on the surface to be taken in by rain during a wet spell will be much the easiest.

For the first four to six weeks after planting, no further feeding should be needed, but from mid-July a moderate feed given every seven days will help. It is far better to give medium-strength feed every seven days than strong feed every ten to fourteen days. There are many proprietary fertilizers available, and it would be foolish of me to recommend any specific one, but I favour one with an analysis of approximately 9 per cent nitrogen, 5 per cent soluble phosphoric acid and 4 per cent potash plus trace elements. Any subsequent adjustment of the nitrogen-potash content can, as previously stated, be made with the development of the plant. Feeding is continued up to and including the period of securing buds and, furthermore, until the time when the cellophane-like skin of the bud splits to show its first tinge of colour. After this two further feeds are necessary, given at weekly intervals at weak strength instead of medium. After this feeding is stopped. There will be critics of this high nitrogenous type of feeding and probably one or two seasons are necessary to master it. The gardener wishing to grow only for garden decoration and cut-flowers will not wish to resort to the necessary study and record-keeping required by the keen exhibitor. In such cases, if the ground has been well prepared as suggested, a sprinkling of dry fertilizer around plants in July and a second in August, to be taken in by the weather, will be more than adequate to give good results. Conversely, you may wish to keep to the more conventional method of feeding, which certainly will still give a fair proportion of red prize tickets, so important to thousands of gardeners throughout the country who, although not primarily classing themselves as exhibitors, still like to make a few entries to support their local shows. Once again, treatment is governed by proper ground preparation but from late June until securing the bud a higher-nitrogen fertilizer is used, one with a nitrogen content of 6–7 per cent which is given every seven to ten days until buds are secured. Feeding is temporarily halted until buds show signs of swelling. Then feeding is recommenced, but from now on the accent is on higher potash, using fertilizers similar to those used in growing tomatoes where potash content will be 7 per cent and nitrogen down to about 3–4 per cent; once colour shows in the bud, feeding stops completely.

It is very likely that with varying types of soil a system of feeding somewhere between these two methods will be adopted. The programme detailed has been based on my own cultivation over twenty-five years on very light soil; a heavier medium will possibly demand some slight adjustment.

Protection

If exhibition plants are being grown, the aim is to produce blooms as near perfect as possible, and it would be foolish not to admit that some form of protection is needed. Quite apart from the weather, there are many parts of the country where industrial fall-out can spoil blooms, and certainly if your gardening takes place in a densely built-up area there is an additional hazard from local bonfire fiends; few neighbourhoods are without one of these.

The simplest form of protection is by double bagging, using grease-proof bags whose seams are fastened with waterproof glue. Although these are cheap, the main drawback in their use is that blooms cannot be seen while they are developing; in addition, although whites and yellows will not suffer, other colours, if bagged too early, lose colour in varying degrees.

Bags can be prepared well in advance to be ready for one of the rush periods of chrysanthemum culture. Because a certain amount of rain seeps through the outer bag, if no remedial action is taken the bottom of the bag gradually collects rain until it becomes too heavy and the bloom heels over. To obviate this, small holes are pierced in the outer bag about 7½cm (3in) up from the neck, to allow rain which seeps through to drain away, leaving the inner bag and the bloom completely dry.

When the outer bags have been prepared, another bag is placed inside each one, with the seam on the opposite side. Initially 25 cm by 25cm (10in by 10in) bags will suffice for a considerable number of medium cultivars, while most large-flowering plants need 30cm by 33cm (12in by 13in) to allow for the much larger blooms.

The time to bag is when buds are beginning to show a faint trace of colour, as young florets burst through the cellophane-like skin which has protected them prior to this stage. Before bagging, buds are sprayed or dusted with insecticide to make sure that there are no aphids present. To place the bag over a bud which is harbouring any insect pest is fatal; the insect, usually some form of aphid, will multiply so rapidly that the developing bloom is rendered useless from the resulting excretion. To avoid this, buds should be well sprayed or dusted with insecticide, allowed to dry, and covered immediately. It often happens that, with a lot of buds showing colour all at once, to give initial protection quickly is not possible as it takes a fair amount of time to fasten large bags into position. If small 10cm (4in) sweet bags are first used these can quickly be fastened with a small twist-it, they can safely be left for ten to fourteen days and then, after removing them and checking that sprays have been effective, larger bags are used to replace them at a more leisurely rate. Before placing a bag over buds, tuck its two corners in and, after gathering the neck between the thumb and forefinger, inflate by blowing into it. Place it over the bud, then gather the neck together about 7½cm (3in) down the stem and tie tightly with green twist or raffia, making sure that the supporting cane is also included with the stem as otherwise the bloom may snap off in strong winds. If the neck of the bag is moistened before use, it will help it to fit tightly around the stem. Often it is necessary to extend the supporting cane. A thinner, split cane is used for this; one end is pushed into the central hole of the stout cane and any surplus length is easily cut with a pair of secateurs. To complete this operation, fasten a loose tie around each plant to hold bags together so that they are just touching one another. Any wind will then cause the bags to sway together as one unit, rather than collide with one another.

Another method of bag protection is to use specially manufactured frames. When unfolded, these have four prongs that fit either into the hole at the end of a bamboo cane or into a plastic tube provided for this purpose, which is fastened to the cane. This offers a more substantial form of protection and a single cloche-type bag with a window down one side is fitted over the frame, giving the added advantage that blooms can be seen developing. Again, this is fastened underneath to both cane and chrysanthemum stem. The more dedicated exhibitor with a large number of blooms to protect will be better served if a more permanent means of covering is erected over complete beds of plants. After devoting months of work to-producing blooms as near as possible to perfection, many in colours which do not lend themselves to bag protection, to leave them at the mercy of the elements is quite unforgivable.

A permanent supporting framework can easily be erected using angle iron or timber. It is better if iron or concrete supports are sunk into the ground; these do not rot as is the case when wood is used throughout. The structure should allow for a height of 2 metres (6½ft) in the centre and 1½ metres (5ft) at the sides; this permits ample circulation of air, so essential once covers are in position. On this framework either polythene covers, sheets of transparent PVC or Dutch lights are fastened, but these must not be placed over plants too early as young buds need maximum light and early morning dews to assist in their development. To cover prematurely is liable to draw up stems, making them thin and leggy, so that they may not be sufficiently strong enough to hold up a good, heavy exhibition bloom. Finally, once the covers are in position, artificial watering will have to be given from then on.

Regulating Growth

A few years ago, the suggestion that growth of plants could be controlled by applying chemicals would have been looked upon with disfavour by the chrysanthemum fraternity. Nowadays, however, keen gardeners will go to great lengths to gain the required results; this is emphasized by the fact that no lecture or question-time panel is complete without a question being asked about some method of height retardent. B9, a chemical regulator first introduced from America, was originally used extensively in growing all-the-year-round chrysanthemums commercially; it was many years before it became available to amateurs. The main effect of B9 is not so much to prevent growth but rather to encourage production of sturdier growth and, in so doing, discourage longitudinal development. This attribute is particularly useful when applied to cultivars which naturally have long, weak-necked stems, sometimes hardly strong enough to hold a fully developed bloom erect.

Some elementary rules, simple enough to follow, must be applied rigidly if success is to be ensured. Unlike many other chemicals used in the culture of various plants, B9 leaves little margin for error. It should never be mixed and applied with an insecticide or fungicide because of possible chemical reaction, but must be applied entirely on its own. It is advisable to apply as a spray only; normal air pressure sprayers are suitable and they should be made of plastic rather than metal as the latter can be affected by chemical reaction. Plants should be crisp and fresh before application and foliage should remain dry for twenty-four hours after spraying to allow the B9 to be absorbed by the leaf tissue, but care must be taken to prevent any surplus spray falling on to the ground as this can adversely affect a plant's root system.

To reduce the length of neck in early-flowering cultivars, B9 at the rate of one part to ten parts of water is sprayed on the top 22½cm (9in) of the plant several days before the final disbudding and securing of the main bud. Tall-growing plants can be controlled by shortening the distance between each set of leaves, but here several applications of a weaker solution must be used from June onwards. As the actual strength and frequency of application are dependent upon the cultivar and growing conditions, experiments will once more be necessary, but as a guide, if a solution of one part B9 to one hundred parts of water is sprayed on at four-weekly intervals during June, July and August, results should be satisfactory; in this case the whole plant is sprayed.

Late greenhouse cultivars are notoriously tall growers and much assistance can be given in reducing the height of plants if the system of frequent applications as described for earlies is used. Alternatively, the following method reduces plants by 30–45cm (12–18in)— a considerable reduction when the plant might otherwise reach a height of 2¼ metres (approx 7ft). At the time of potting on into a 15cm (6in) pot, B9 at the strength of one part to twenty-five parts of water is sprayed on the plant, to be followed by a second spray of the same strength when breaks are about 30–45cm (12–18in) in length. It is possible that many different strengths and times of application of B9 will prove equally effective, but caution should be used with red, bronze and pink cultivars as some interference with the red pigment can be experienced. This artificial shortening of stems greatly assists gardeners with small greenhouses who otherwise would not be able to grow many of the lovely late cultivars.

This important phase of chrysanthemum culture has been dealt with fully in chapter 7, which it is advisable to re-read at this point. While many individual operations can be varied according to the needs of the grower, there are no short cuts to timing procedure if blooms are to be harvested before the bad autumn weather sets in.

Spraying

From the outset, a regular spraying programme against pests and diseases must be established. To wait until signs of damage or an infestation are visible is certainly not worthwhile; the old adage that prevention is better than cure, was never more apt than when applied to control of the troubles that can, through neglect, beset chrysanthemum growers. Fortunately many excellent insecticides and fungicides are available to assist us, so there is no need to be deterred by the thoughts of disease being so rife that it is not worth bothering with chrysanthemum growing to any great extent.

Good husbandry in itself will go a long way towards avoiding a lot of trouble. An untidy garden where rubbish is left around, or weeds allowed to grow, furnishes many pests with host plants and excellent conditions for breeding. Strong healthy plants, like humans, are far more resistant to disease than weak ones, so for a good chance of success only the best must be planted.

Although individual pests and diseases are dealt with fully in chapter 11, it would be fatal to imagine that the slightest discoloration of foliage is due to some virus disease or that one damaged floret in a bloom means the garden has been invaded by an army of earwigs. The subject of spraying must always be kept in its proper perspective: regular spraying is necessary in any garden, as most people will know from having seen greenfly on roses or blackfly on runner beans, and chrysanthemums are no exception.

Generally, my own system is to spray plants every seven to ten days on a rota system using three different ingredients: BHC, Malathion and Pirimor. The reason is twofold: first there is no single all-purpose spray which controls every known pest; second, it has been proved beyond all possible doubt that certain pests build up a higher resistance to some insecticides and it is therefore logical to ring the changes. Chrysanthemum mildew, the most common disease, is controlled by a monthly application of copper mildew specific or the more modern fungicide Benlate, containing the systemic fungicide Benomyl.

Systemic insecticides and fungicides are comparatively new introductions for use by amateurs, though they have been used commercially for many years. Briefly, they rely upon absorption by the plant for their effectiveness and, in the case of insecticides, remain active for several weeks. Sap-sucking insects are killed by the presence of insecticide in minute quantities in the plant tissue. Unfortunately the main systemic insecticide, Metasystox, is particularly toxic, although it is true that there is no danger if the recommended precautions are followed to the letter. These involve protecting bare skin, using a mask and only applying the insecticide on a very still day. A considerable amount of danger can be overcome if, instead of using a fine spray, the insecticide is watered over plants from a fine-rosed Hawes-type watering can. Because of the long spout on these cans, if they are held at arm's length it is possible to be at a fairly safe distance from the insecticide as it is applied. It will now be obvious that systemics are only recommended for ardent chrysanthemum growers who are prepared and willing to follow these detailed instructions. Ordinary gardeners are probably well-advised to keep to the safer types of insecticides.

Lifting and Storing

The hardiness of modern outdoor chrysanthemums has become distinctly suspect over the years as new cultivars have been developed. Increased inter-breeding using late greenhouse cultivars for cross-pollination, plus modern methods of bombarding cuttings and seed with gamma radiation, have helped to interfere with the course of nature, and this interference is likely to continue while there is a continual demand for the introduction of new cultivars. One side-effect of this is lack of hardiness in many cultivars. If the winter is comparatively mild, it should be quite possible to leave plants in the open ground, but there are other important considerations which must be taken into account. Heavy losses can be experienced from excessive damp conditions or the ravages of slugs; but the final problem, and indeed a very vital one, is that if plants are left in the ground it is impossible to prepare the soil adequately for the following season. If only a few plants are being grown in borders, a gamble can be taken on the weather and plants lifted and divided in the early spring, but this course of action is hardly suitable for the keen gardener.

As a prelude to lifting, selection of clean healthy stock is essential. During the growing season, plants of cultivars it is proposed to retain which have produced good blooms should be marked in an easily identifiable manner. Similarly, a sub-standard plant should be pulled up and destroyed as soon as any fault is noticed; yellowing foliage, wilting and malformed blooms are all possible signs of disease or genetic breakdown and to propagate from such plants would only carry the trouble over to another season.

Many growers do not possess a greenhouse or cold frame, but they should still lift their plants and a little improvisation can assist in bringing the boxed plants through the winter.

The first very obvious choice is a large box with a sheet of glass over the top in a sheltered part of the garden, but this almost comes within the category of a cold frame. There is a great temptation to put boxes of stools in sheds or garages, but the danger from lack of light is almost as bad as that from frost. Fortunately, a compromise can be reached: if boxes are stood in a sheltered part of the garden and protected from heavy rain, they can easily be lifted into a shed at night if frost threatens and put out again the next day. However, for serious growing a cold frame should be considered as an essential item of equipment and the rest of my advice is based on the assumption that you either have a cold frame or will obtain one before serious growing is commenced.

It is unwise to lift stools too early as they benefit from partial rest under cooler autumn conditions, allowing the sap to die down in the main stem. As early as possible after blooms have been harvested, cut down main stems leaving 20–30cm (8–12in) on the plant; this makes it less likely to bleed in storage, so avoiding the risk of mildew forming. At this stage any basal growths around the main stem can be allowed to develop and flower. These supply excellent sprays of intense colour, very suitable for cut-flower and indoor decoration. Over the years I have found that the period from mid-October to mid-November is the best time for lifting; this allows sufficient time for the job to be completed before bad weather sets in.

To lift stools, a small border fork, often referred to as a lady's fork, is pushed into the ground 15cm (6in) away from the main stem on three sides to help loosen the roots. The plant is eased out of the ground from the fourth side. All basal growths are now cut down to ground level and any coarse roots are trimmed off with sharp secateurs. While there are varying schools of thought on whether or not old soil should be washed off stools, it is rather a long process and does not give any extra guarantees. Personally, I am of the opinion that if stock has been watched, looked after throughout the season and finally selected, there is no reason or need to resort to washing all the old soil away; instead, just the top thin layer of soil is removed as this often tends to get a little green or scummy during the growing season.

Stools are now placed in shallow trays about 7½cm (3in) deep; the familiar tomato trays are ideal for this purpose. The number of stools per tray varies according to size of the root system, but will range between four plants for strong-growing cultivars, and up to eight or ten with weaker ones. If space permits, it is as well to keep one cultivar to each box; but if more than one cultivar is put into a box or tray, firm wooden divisions to separate them are required in order to avoid cuttings of different cultivars growing into one another and causing confusion when propagating time comes round.

Once stools are fitted into the trays, spaces in between are filled with compost such as John Innes No 1, or, as an alternative, equal parts by bulk of moist peat, John Innes No 1 and sand, well mixed together. After firming with the fingers, a light watering is given with a fine-rosed can; no further watering should be needed until after Christmas. A dusting over the surface with insecticide powder, plus a few slug pellets, will look after possible attacks of most pests. As a precaution it is as well to dust the top of the cut-down main stem with yellow flowers of sulphur to prevent any mildew spores forming. The accent now is on cool airy conditions to avoid any possibility of a damp atmosphere. A cold frame is the best place in which to stand the boxes and if a layer of weathered ashes or very sharp sand is first put on the ground in the frame, it will help to deter slugs from penetrating through to the boxes.

Under these conditions the stools will remain practically dormant, but regular checks must be made to renew slug bait when necessary and to make sure that mildew is not forming on the stems.

Starting Growth

During late December or early January, the boxes are transferred from the cold frame into the greenhouse, placed on the staging, and given a watering with a fine-rosed can. High temperatures are not needed as this only leads to spindly growth being made, hardly suitable for making good cuttings. A temperature of 7–10°C (45–50°F) is ideal, and will soon lead to the production of a good crop of new growths ready to use as cuttings. Even at this early stage in the year, a routine spray must be given to prevent pests taking shelter in the new growths. Once these growths begin to extend as a result of warmer conditions in the greenhouse, everything will be ready to start actual propagation.

9 *Cultivation of Late Greenhouse Cultivars*

Potting

The treatment of greenhouse cultivars after the initial potting stage is vastly different from that described for early-flowering types. While they also spend the summer months outdoors, late-flowering chrysanthemums have to be moved on into larger pots to enable them to be lifted into a greenhouse during the second half of September for flowering during late October, November and December.

SECOND POTTING

Once rooted, cuttings of late-flowering chrysanthemums are moved into small pots or boxes as detailed in chapter 6. Up to this point they will have been treated exactly the same as earlies but, unlike earlies which are planted directly into open ground, lates need to be potted on as the food supply in small pots soon becomes exhausted. Depending upon the size of the root system and the vigour of individual plants, either a 12½cm (5in) or 15cm (6in) pot will be used.

It may be asked why this extra work is necessary; why not move plants straight from a 7½cm (3in) pot into the final size pot? The answer is simple: if a plant was transferred in such a way in one move, the root system would not be large enough to penetrate quickly into the very much larger bulk of compost. The compost would in all probability remain much too moist and become sour, with detrimental effects on the plant.

It is difficult to decide whether a plant is ready for this move simply by inspecting the development of its foliage; so it is necessary from early March for inspections of the root systems to be made every few days to determine if any plant is ready for its move. This is not a job which can be done indiscriminately; lates do demand individual treatment and if this is not given, then like spoilt prima donnas they will show their resentment at not being studied properly.

Fortunately, if the compost in the pots has been watered the previous evening, examination is simple enough. Holding the plant with its stem between the fingers, the pot is inverted and then, with a light tap of the rim on the edge of bench or staging, the ball of roots will come away easily.

If the roots are breaking through the compost, while those at the bottom are just beginning to circle round, then the plant is ready for moving on; at all events, plants must not be allowed to become pot-bound, as in this condition plant food soon becomes exhausted and the foliage quickly takes on a distinct yellow colour.

Having decided on the correct size of pot, a small crock is placed over the central drainage hole and then covered with some fibrous compost. On top of this, place a layer of John Innes No 2 compost, knock the plant out of the smaller pot and carefully place the ball of roots centrally in the larger prepared pot. Fresh compost is now gradually added and firmed with the fingers so that when potting is finished, although the old ball of roots is covered, there is still about 1½cm (½in) of space between the soil and the rim of the pot to allow for watering. A short cane is inserted and the plant is fastened to it.

It will be impossible to return the larger pots to the protection of a cold frame so they are now stood close together in a sheltered place to allow for further hardening-off to take place; watering must only be given when absolutely necessary and then only through a fine-rosed can. The difficulty here is to achieve a happy medium: the roots of a waterlogged plant will soon die; on the other hand, if too little water is given, the compost becomes dry, a slight gap due to shrinkage of the compost will form between the compost and the pot and if this happens it will mean that water will run straight through the pot leaving the centrally-placed root system high and dry. If this gap should occur, firm slightly around the edges with a potting stick to seal up the gap.

FINAL POTTING

Towards the end of May and early in June, another move into large final pots is required. Here again an inspection of the rooting system will be needed, and a decision must be made regarding the size of final pot to be used. The correct pot, according to the plant's root development, is of the utmost importance, and although there may be a certain amount of latitude, over- or under-potting can both have equally bad effects on plants during their season of growth. With experience, choice will very soon become a sixth sense; however, as a guide, which must be taken very generally, large exhibition types need 22–25cm (8½–10in), medium exhibition, exhibition incurves, decoratives and large singles 22cm (8½in) and medium singles 19–22cm (7½–8½in). The only other advice which can be given to less experienced growers is, if any doubt exists with a cultivar in its first season of growth, use a slightly smaller rather than a larger pot and be guided by results for adjustment in its next season. The question of whether plastic or clay pots should be used is often the subject of heated discussion, as both have their devotees. A lot depends upon how a grower commences; both types of pot give excellent results, but differences in use are so important that switching from the older clay pot system is quite difficult. One great difference is that, due to the porous nature of clay pots, watering is required more frequently than when using plastic ones, but such differences can soon be mastered with practice. One very big advantage of the plastic pot is its comparatively light weight which, when used in conjunction with soil-less compost, enables disabled or elderly people, who would be unable to lift heavy weights, still to carry on the wonderful hobby of growing all the lovely greenhouse cultivars. The use of soil-less compost was fully discussed in chapter 4.

The majority of growers of late greenhouse cultivars still prefer to use clay pots and potting media vary considerably from grower to grower, ranging from own mixtures to ready-mixed John Innes compost. There is a great deal to be said in praise of John Innes compost, provided it is obtained from a reputable supplier who uses good quality loam in the mixture. Beginners are advised to keep to the John Innes formula using the No 4 mixture; other composts can be experimented with once experience has been gained, but only then if results have not been up to standard. Change for the sake of change seldom brings better blooms; change because results are below standard may often produce improvement. The same procedure is followed for this final potting as was detailed for the move into 12½cm or 15cm (5in or 6in) pots; the only exception is the use of a potting stick, since a larger amount of compost is to be added. Concrete-like conditions are not required, though slightly firmer potting is recommended for incurved cultivars. The aim should be to have a degree of firmness in the new compost when potting is finished equal to that in the ball of roots of the plant from the smaller pot. When completed, the level of the compost should be approximately

6cm (2½in) below the rim of the pot to allow for top dressing later in the season.

Watering is seldom required immediately after final potting, unless the weather is very hot and dry. Compost should not be allowed to become too dry at this stage; otherwise, as mentioned previously, when water is given it will run straight through without moistening the main ball of roots. Until roots have penetrated the new compost and the surface has been consolidated, watering must be done with a fine-rosed can to avoid making a hole or washing compost out of the pot. Pots are now stood close together for two to three weeks. They are watered when necessary, subjected to spraying against pests, and protected from the attention of birds by black cotton wound around canes. If soil-less compost has been used, some arrangement will have to be made to fasten supporting canes as, unlike soil compost, the medium is loose and will not hold canes erect without support.

STANDING GROUND

After the plants have been in their final pots for about three weeks, they are ready to be moved to the standing ground they will occupy during the summer and early autumn until the time comes to house them in the greenhouse. This standing ground should be in as open a position as possible, so that plants can get maximum light and air. Above all, there must be ample room so that plants will not be overcrowded. Firm supports are needed and these are best provided by driving solid posts or steel pipes into the ground 2–3 metres (6–9ft) apart. On the posts, two strainer wires are fastened about 1 metre (3ft) and 1½ metres (5ft) from the ground. A layer of weathered ashes or sharp sand is spread on the ground on which the pots are stood, supporting canes being fastened to the straining wires. Thinning down breaks to the number of stems required giving them each an individual cane, stopping and disbudding, as previously explained will proceed during June and possibly into early July. Watering, however, is very different from that of early-flowering cultivars in open ground.

Watering

Chrysanthemums in pots can be very fussy in their water requirements because of the small volume of soil, the very different root systems and varying rates of evaporation between small- and large-leaved cultivars; individual treatment must therefore be given whenever possible. The art of pot watering really involves a sixth sense as experience is gained. The fact that composts used can be divided into two main types—soil-based or soil-less peat composts—means that very different treatment is required in each case when it comes to watering. With soil composts the first piece of general advice is, if in doubt as to whether to water or not, leave it until the next day. On the other hand, with peat-based composts the process must be completely reversed, as the compost should always be kept slightly moist; if allowed to dry out it is very difficult to water effectively again, as anyone who has tried to moisten a bale of dry peat will know.

It is always detrimental to over-water, but the most dangerous time to over-water pots is during the first few weeks after final potting. Once the root system has increased so that it has a firm hold in the bulk of compost, the danger is very much less. Rain absorbed by pots can be very misleading, especially when plants develop larger foliage later in the season, when a considerable amount of rain is likely to be deflected from the pots by leaves. In fact, it is almost possible to ignore rain unless it falls heavily enough to be classified as a storm. The only observation I would make here is that during prolonged rainy spells there is naturally less evaporation from the top of the pot, and certainly very much less transpiration through the sides of the pot, which in itself restricts the need for watering too frequently.

From the end of June onwards it will be advisable to make daily inspections, except perhaps in a period of very dull, cool weather. The only sure indication with clay pots is the old-fashioned pot-tapping method: pots requiring water give a distinctive ring, due to the very slight air space between compost and the outer edges of the pot; while a dull thud indicates the pot has plenty of water in it. It is difficult to use this system with both peat-based composts and plastic pots, and here there is no accepted method; but fortunately there is not quite the same element of danger in over-watering.

Most gardeners, experienced or otherwise, regard any wilting of established plants as being the first sign of the need for watering, but when dealing with chrysanthemums, whether grown in the open ground or pot-grown plants, there are at least two occasions when wilting in all probability does not indicate the need for watering. If there is a period of dull or wet weather, even if only for a few days' duration, followed by a sudden burst of hot sunny weather, plants will hang quite limp even though the ground or the compost in the pot is moist. This reaction is probably due to certain chemical changes taking place in the cells of the plant and it would be very wrong to water. Another time when the extreme tips of plants wilt and hang their heads is just before buds are secured. Once the main bud begins to swell after it has been secured, the tendency to wilt under these weather conditions disappears; here again no extra watering is needed, but if plants and the surrounding ground area are lightly hosed or sprayed with water in the early evening following a very hot day, they will greatly benefit from such treatment.

One further word of warning, allied to both watering and standing ground; if pots are placed on a smooth surface, small particles of soil gradually form a seal around the bottom of the pot which can, if left, inhibit drainage and in some instances may lead to complete waterlogging. If it is not possible to stand pots on a rough, well-drained surface, they should be moved slightly once a week to prevent this barrier forming.

Feeding

For first-class results, it has been more than adequately proved that a careful diet, properly administered, will give improved blooms when cultivating chrysanthemums. The need for this balanced feeding is no doubt more essential with greenhouse cultivars than with early outdoor plants, because of the leaching of nutrients from pots as a result of continuous watering throughout the season. Feeding methods, the fertilizers used, the method of application and even the various accents on higher nitrogen or higher potash fertilizers differ between growers: ultimately there may be little difference in the end product, but this is without doubt due to the willingness of growers to study, experiment and find a sequence of operations which suits their particular conditions and methods.

Gardeners who do not wish to exhibit but nevertheless enjoy producing good blooms for use in the home during November and December can manage with three feeds during July and August at two-weekly intervals. A proprietary solid feed at one dessertspoonful per plant each feed, sprinkled on the surface of the compost to be taken when watering will be sufficient.

Keen growers, possibly with exhibiting in mind, require a more detailed programme and although the following may sound excessive, it has been well tried and tested without any ill effects. Some additional nitrogen feed, according to the season, may well be contemplated. Indeed, this can be given, but a warning must be registered:

take it gently and carefully; high nitrogen, wrongly applied, can be damaging to plants if an excess is used. If one or two plants are retained on normal feed as controls when experimenting, a great deal will be learnt about the production of super-blooms. For a month after final potting, plants find sufficient food contained in their new compost, but directly these few weeks have passed the time is right for supplementary feeding. At this stage our concern is to keep vegetative growth moving; but while over-lush plants may look very nice they seldom produce blooms of size and quality so our endeavours must be to try and reach a state of good growth and reasonable ripeness. In this condition, as with earlies, plants are not so susceptible to damage if slightly higher nitrogen feed is given from time to time.

Much depends on weather conditions and personal choice as to whether solid or liquid fertilizers are used but a combination of both would seem to be most logical. About the middle of July, a start is made with a teaspoonful (5ml) of Bentley's No 1. This contains 4·9 per cent nitrogen and 3·6 per cent potash, and is sprinkled around each plant at mid-week. In addition, water with medium-strength liquid fertilizer at the weekend. During the months of August and September, until buds are secured, increase the Bentley's to a dessertspoonful per plant each week and the liquid fertilizer to full strength. Once buds are secured, Bentleys No 2 containing 7·5 per cent nitrogen and 3·6 per cent potash is substituted for No 1, while the liquid fertilizer is kept at full strength. As soon as buds begin to show colour, the Bentley's is reduced back to a teaspoonful per plant and the liquid feed to half strength for two weeks only; if this coincides with housing, the feeding can still be carried on in the greenhouse. At the end of two weeks the solid feed is stopped completely, but liquid feeding is continued whenever watering or foliar spray is required until blooms are harvested. In addition to the feeding programme described, a watering of sulphate of magnesium (Epsom salts) is given once during July and again in August; this assists in giving an intensity of colour in foliage and blooms.

Mention has been made of possible higher nitrogen feed, provided plants are sufficiently ripe in the wood to receive it. This can be supplied in a form that will be quickly absorbed by plants if urea is used at 5ml (1 teaspoonful) to one gallon of water for four to six plants. The frequency of its application must be governed by the weather and condition of plants but remembering that urea contains 46 per cent nitrogen I would suggest that it is not given more than once every two weeks from early July to late August. Once more it must be emphasized that careful use is advised at first, and that on no account should urea be used indiscriminately.

Top Dressing

There is an additional way of assisting plants to their maximum potential by means of top dressing, using the space left at the top of the pots when final potting was done. This area is filled up in stages with more compost which, if the time of application of solid feed, as suggested in the feeding programme, is due, can include the fertilizer together with the compost when added.

The compost can be similar to that used for final potting and is given in dressings of approximately 1cm ($\frac{1}{2}$in) each time in mid-July and early August. After each dressing, any necessary watering should be done with a fine-rosed can until the surface has been consolidated again. The benefit of this top dressing is threefold: it feeds existing roots, encourages new roots to grow into the fresh compost so increasing the root system and finally it has been proved that plants which have been top dressed usually produce a better crop of basal shoots for use as cuttings when needed for propagation purposes.

Housing

The time to transfer late-flowering chrysanthemums into the greenhouse depends entirely upon prevailing weather conditions and a plant's stage of bud development. Once the buds are showing colour it will need protection; but if the weather is warm and sunny, the temperature in the greenhouse is likely to be on the high side and will not be suitable, so temporary protection can be given to the bud by fastening a small bag over it with a twist-it. However, unless it is a yellow or white cultivar, housing can only be delayed for seven to ten days; otherwise the developing florets will begin to lose colour. Except for the odd large exhibition plant, there is usually no need to commence housing before the second or third week of September. Indeed, while buds are swelling there is no doubt that these benefit from the September dews, but once the cellophane-like skin begins to break housing will become quite urgent.

While waiting to house plants, there is a lot of preparation to be done to the greenhouse. If another crop, such as tomatoes, has been grown during the summer months, it must first be cleared out and all debris removed. The house must now be thoroughly washed down with soapy water to which disinfectant has been added, followed by rinsing or hosing down with clean water. Ventilators and door are left open and once the house is dry any necessary repairs should be effected; particular attention is given to any possibility of leaky roof ventilators or glazing bars.

In most seasons some form of shading will be needed, as the sun can be quite fierce at times, even in October. There is nothing, in my opinion, to beat curtains made of butter muslin which can be drawn or pushed back when necessary; it is much easier to fasten them into position when the house is empty rather than leave them until the plants have been installed. The curtains can also be drawn at night to protect blooms from any condensation which may drip down; at the same time protection will be given to the florets, which often damp slightly if exposed to the early morning sun.

If adjustable curtains cannot be fixed there is no option but to use a light form of permanent shading and the recently introduced product called Coolglass is extremely effective. White in colour, it is supplied in the form of a thick cream which, when mixed with water, can be brushed or sprayed on the outside of the glass. Although the heaviest of storms does not wash this shading off, at the end of the season it is easily wiped off with a duster.

HEATING

Heating apparatus is the next item to need attention, as it tends to be neglected during the summer months. While some fortunate growers have piped heat from a boiler, various forms of electrical heating are probably the most popular. A fan heater is ideally suited to chrysanthemum culture, as gentle heat plus movement of air gives the correct environment for proper development of blooms; in particular, the very large exhibition blooms must have this circulation of air if problems of damping florets are to be avoided. To this end, in conjunction with heating, one or two additional cool fans, set higher in the roof of the house to blow a cool stream of air over the developing blooms, should help to keep everything trouble-free.

SUBSEQUENT TREATMENT

Once flowering is finished, attention must be given to plants to encourage the production of suitable growths to use as cuttings for the new season. Main stems, as with early-flowering cultivars, are cut down, canes are removed and surface of the compost is lightly pricked over. Surrounding basal growths are cut down but, as new cuttings will be wanted very much earlier, existing basal growths are only shortened to the last pair of leaves above soil level. This is done as a precaution, so that if new basal growths do not push through the compost suitable side-shoots will grow from the leaf axils of these cut-down growths. When plants have been cut down, staging should be erected as soon as possible in the greenhouse and pots moved up from the floor to obtain maximum light; if left on the floor, new growths would probably grow spindly and be completely unsuitable for good cuttings. Stock selection plays a large part in greenhouse cultivation and plants intended for propagation are marked during the growing season. They must be meticulously selected; no plant should be retained if the slightest defect manifests itself in either bloom or foliage.

I have detailed the method practised by many growers who, with only a minimum number of pots, do not have to worry too much about space; but large pots take up a considerable amount of room, especially when trays of earlies have also to be accommodated in the greenhouse prior to propagation. The answer is to turn plants out of their large pots and either wash off old soil and put plants into boxes with fresh compost, or slice off the bottom half of the plant, trim the four sides and then box up. If this is done immediately flowering has finished, it may well lead to a much greater crop of cuttings.

10 *Cultivation of Pot Plants*

There are many late-flowering types of chrysanthemums very suitable for pot culture, ranging from a delightful strain of dwarf pot plants first raised at the University of London College at Wye in Kent, to the very large specimen plants, carrying 150 to 250 blooms, which are admired so much at the National Chrysanthemum Society shows in London during November. These all demand a certain amount of devotion to detail but equally the basic principles of cultivation are reasonably easy.

Specimen Plants

Before embarking on the cultivation of a specimen plant it would be as well to study the definition as laid down by the National Chrysanthemum Society, as these are mainly grown as plants entirely for exhibition purposes.

A specimen plant should have a large number of high quality blooms and an abundance of clean, healthy foliage. The plant must be on a single stem and there should be at least one inch of main stem clear of the soil below the first branch or break. The training or bending of the stems should begin near the base and not near the blooms. Canes, framework and ties must also be unobtrusive, and individual blooms displayed to the best advantage.

When undertaking the cultivation of one of these monsters, it must be realized that it calls for considerable care and attention for all twelve months of the year. A vital requirement is a means of protection during the flowering period, which demands a greenhouse or conservatory with doors wide enough to allow for housing the plant. Remembering that it may grow to 1½ metres (5ft) in diameter, ample door space becomes a very necessary consideration. An alternative to greenhouse protection is a polythene-covered framework which can be made to lift easily over the plant, affording protection against the weather from September to November. Facilities must be provided to secure the framework to the ground; otherwise strong winds will soon blow it away and damage the plant.

The choice of a suitable cultivar must now be made and this is very strictly limited by certain requirements. For this type of culture the plant needs to be capable of producing many breaks and at the same time taking up to three or four stoppings, without too much loss of size in the final blooms. Some years ago 'Annie Curry' and 'Golden Curry' were preferred, and these are still used by some growers, but now the 'Princess Anne' family and 'Connie Mayhew' are widely used. Possibly 'Yellow' or 'Golden Princess Anne' looks most effective because of its lovely intense colour.

To allow sufficient time for the required number of stoppings, cuttings must be struck during November so that they are rooted by December in time for their first stopping. Normal procedure is followed for taking cuttings, though it is more convenient to place them singly in a $7\frac{1}{2}$cm (3in) pot; then, once rooting has taken place, subsequent pottings are made until the final $45\frac{1}{2}$cm (18in) size is reached. This last potting is by no means easy, as the plant by this time will be quite large and heavy. Certainly it will need two people to complete this final potting. All potting should be finished by early June and the compost for the final pot must be rich to sustain such a large plant; John Innes No 4 mixture is to be recommended.

The first stopping is made during December when the plant is about 25cm (10in) high; this may have to be left until early January if the plant is not sufficiently developed in time. From this first stop, as many breaks as possible should be retained. It is very unlikely that there will be more than three or four really good strong breaks so early on and it is pointless to keep any weak growths. When these breaks have grown about 15cm (6in) in length a second stopping is given and once more as many strong even breaks as possible are retained: this will be in the range of three to six per stem. At this stage the plant will usually have in the region of twelve to eighteen breaks. During the early part of June, a third stopping is made and from this four to six further breaks per stem should be obtained; this will mean that the total number of stems will now be in the region of sixty to eighty. For maximum effect, specimen plants rely on a mass of evenly matured blooms so that a fourth and final stop must be given if possible before mid-July, as this then furnishes us with a plant having two hundred or more blooms when it finally flowers.

10 Bud of early flowering plant ready for protection by bagging

11 Incurved blooms

12 Royal Horticultural Society's Trial Ground at Wisley

13 Stopping

14 Early flowering plants ready for planting out

15 Rooted cuttings boxed-on

16 Intermediate blooms

17 Reflexed blooms

18 Pompons

19 Sprays

20 Charm – Golden Chalice

From the outset, training and tying in growths must be carried out every few days so that young stems can be bent while pliable, in order that at maturity we have a good dome-shaped form to the plant. Canes of varying lengths will be used at first until the growths are sufficiently long for a wire umbrella-like framework to be fitted into place. It is then a question of re-tying in the breaks on to this framework with green twist.

To ensure complete, even development, the pot must be given a slight turn each day so that every part of the plant obtains its full share of light. With very large plants watering can be a problem, especially in hot weather, as they must never be allowed to dry out. Although water may be given in the morning, often by midday a second watering is necessary, and perhaps, on some days, even a third in the late afternoon; so caring for the plant has to be a family affair.

With the copious amounts of water given, the nutrient content of the final potting compost quickly becomes exhausted. Feeding must therefore be commenced early in July, using a solid feed to be taken in with the watering. There are many chrysanthemum fertilizers which can be used, but I still favour Bentley's No 1, given at the rate of a heaped tablespoonful every seven days, changing to Bentley's No 2 in mid-August with an additional watering of Epsom salts, one teaspoonful to the gallon, during July.

Spraying is another task which must be maintained from the initial cutting stage as part of normal routine. The only other control is to keep the plant free of superfluous side-shoots and securing the final buds on each stem. As with individual blooms, clusters of small buds will appear, and the great art is to ensure that the restriction is practised to such a high degree that buds will develop uniformly over the whole plant.

Charms

Spectacular, bush-like charm chrysanthemums are always admired. Their habit, size and mass of Michaelmas-daisy-type blooms make them ideal for house or conservatory decoration. Developed from experiments with seed originating in China, their appearance is so beautiful that many gardeners often think charms must be exceedingly difficult to grow; but they can be raised from seed, struck as cuttings from stock plants or purchased as young rooted plants, all of which will flower in their first season. Seed is sown during late January/early February in a cool greenhouse and when seedlings are large enough to handle these are pricked out singly into 7½cm (3in) pots.

Propagation from cuttings follows the accepted method of taking cuttings as previously described. They are taken slightly later than the date on which seed is sown, but should still be struck no later than the third week of February and again, once rooted, are moved into a 7½cm (3in) pot. From now on treatment will be the same for both methods of propagation. By the end of April or early May, plants are moved into a 12½cm (5in) pot and stood outside as soon as the danger of frosts has passed. During June, a further move, following the same pattern for all late cultivars, is needed. The final pot size will depend on the strength of the root system but it will be very rare indeed for it to exceed 22½cm (9in). It cannot be stressed too much that too large a pot at any period of growth will not lead to a good plant, in fact in the final stage, if roots are slightly pot-bound, they will be in the right condition to accept the watering that the size of plant demands.

The only restriction needed in their growth is a single stopping when plants are 15cm (6in) high to encourage the production of side shoots if the plants have not already made a natural break; neither further stopping nor disbudding is needed, as the plant will send out a multitude of wiry growths all of which terminate in a group of flower buds.

Side growths or breaks are so firm as they develop that the plant will be virtually self-supporting, but a few short canes may sometimes be necessary to help keep it in a good shape. These canes are allowed to be retained when exhibiting charms, but they should not be visible. Green-dyed split canes about 60cm (2ft) in length are excellent for this purpose. Charms are not gross feeders, but with a plant of this size and the constant watering needed for a comparatively small pot from the end of June onwards, some supplementary feeding is necessary. Feeding does not demand the study of various elements and compounds to the same degree as that of more conventional late-flowering chrysanthemums, and if a watering of weak liquid manure is given once every seven days during July, August and September this should be quite sufficient. Any well-balanced fertilizer will do, but my preference in this kind of feeding does sway in favour of a seaweed-based fertilizer fortified with trace elements.

Up to the time of potting into final pots watering must be undertaken with care, but once the plant is established in its final pot, watering will be required almost every day except during periods of dull, cool, rainy weather. On hot sunny days it is very likely that watering twice a day may be necessary, although it will help in such weather if the plant is stood in a plastic saucer so that it can be watered from the bottom as well as the top to avoid any flagging.

There are only two further very important tasks, which must be dealt with right throughout the season. Regular spraying from initial cutting stage to maturity must be given, with particular attention being paid to the underside of the foliage. From the moment that breaks first begin to grow, pots must also be turned slightly every few days; this action becomes increasingly more important as the buds form on terminal shoots. Failure to twist the pot regularly can give some very startling results, the extreme case being a plant having blooms fully out on one side while on the other buds are only just showing colour, completely spoiling a good plant and many months of growth.

Cascades

Regrettably, these most decorative plants are not seen very often, although they are usually featured in display exhibits staged by various local parks departments. As the name implies, they are trained to 'cascade' down in the form of a miniature floral waterfall, but alternatively an upright, fan-shaped effect can also be used. Although grown extensively in China and Japan, they were hardly known outside these countries until after 1930. The well-known firm of Suttons of Reading did much to introduce them into Britain and in recent years they have played a very important part in the superb decorative exhibits staged by the Slough Parks Department at the National Chrysanthemum Society's late shows in London. Generally the cultivation programme for taking cuttings and the potting sequence closely follow those recommended for late decoratives. Cuttings are struck in January and the final potting is effected in late May, when a rich compost is used. From the end of June, a balanced liquid feed is given twice a week throughout the season and, as with charms, watering is of the utmost importance.

Training for the cascade effect is obtained by restricting the plant at a very early stage to one or two leading growths and then, after standing the pot on a tall shelf or stand facing south, every few days the leading shoots are tied to a cane secured at an angle from the pot down to the ground. In September, plants are housed in the greenhouse ready for flowering in October or November. It is not easy to accommodate these plants, whose flowering leads can be 1½–2 metres (5–6ft) in length when housed, but in a large greenhouse or conservatory it should be possible to fix a shelf fairly high up on which to stand the pot. If a pedestal can be made, so much the better, but the sight of a multitude of flowers cascading down will more than repay the work involved during the season.

Dwarf Pot Plants

No doubt you will have seen dwarf-flowering chrysanthemums in pots, and probably bought some, only to be disappointed the following season when, after propagation, resulting plants have been very tall. The reason for this is that the original plants have probably been artificially dwarfed by controlled manipulation of light and temperature or by the use of chemicals.

While the controlled heat and light conditions necessary for dwarfing may not always be obtainable, it is quite possible for amateurs to raise dwarf plants in a similar manner using a chemical powder known as Phosfon. This is added to potting compost in tiny quantities and results can be very worthwhile.

The versatile 'Princess Anne' family can once more be used for this type of culture and again the yellow sport seems to have the greatest appeal.

The first requirement is a supply of rooted cuttings in September and stock plants are necessary for this purpose, either by rooting cuttings in March or arranging for delivery of some rooted plants from a nurseryman in early May. When received, these plants are planted in a cold frame as this will probably be the most convenient place for them at this time of year.

When plants are approximately 25cm (10in) in height, the tips are pinched out to encourage side-shoots which in turn are prevented from flowering by pinching again. This pinching is continued up to the end of July, so that there are plenty of suitable side-shoots available in early September to use for cuttings.

Cuttings are taken in the conventional way during the month of September, using equal parts John Innes potting compost No 1, peat and sand as a rooting medium. No heating is required at this time of the year as the greenhouse temperature is sufficiently high to give rooting in fourteen days. Meanwhile, compost for potting on the rooted cuttings is prepared. Here 15gm (½oz) of Phosfon is mixed into 36 litres (1 bushel) of compost, the latter being equal parts of John Innes No 2, compost and peat. The chief difficulty is to ensure even distribution of such a small amount of chemical in a comparatively large amount of compost. This is easily overcome if the Phosfon powder is put into an old pepper pot and, after spreading the compost out as much as possible over a flat concrete area, it is sprinkled with the powder, turning it over several times and repeating this treatment until the pepper pot is empty. The treated compost is now ready for immediate use; or, if necessary, it can be stored without loss through chemical activity. This quantity is suitable for about twenty-five shallow 12½cm (5in) pots, plastic pots being very useful for this purpose.

At the end of September the rooted cuttings are potted, five to each pot, using the treated compost. The only precaution necessary is to use rubber gloves for handling the compost and any exposed skin must be washed immediately after using the Phosfon. Care must also be taken not to contaminate ponds, and any receptacles used in the mixing, such as the pepper pot, must also be sterilized with hot water. By mid-October the plants should be about 10cm (4in) high and a stopping is given. Three breaks are allowed to grow from each plant, so that when terminal buds form and are secured, each pot will have fifteen blooms whose stems probably will not exceed 30cm (12in) in length.

In all respects, apart from treating the compost with Phosfon, normal cultural practices are followed. The pots, being on the small side, soon become full of roots, but there will be no deterioration in the plants provided all necessary watering is in the form of a weak liquid feed.

Wye Chrysanthemums

An entirely new race of natural dwarf-growing pot chrysanthemums has been bred by Alan A. Jackson of Wye College, to whom I am indebted for supplying and allowing me to include the information in this book. Basically, a dwarf pot plant is produced from a single cutting without disbudding or the use of a growth regulator. Given one stopping, it makes a balanced plant which is flowered in a 9cm (3½in) pot in about ten weeks from the taking of the cutting, provided that a temperature of 15°C (60°F) is maintained and a twelve-hour period of darkness is given.

Mature plants are only 22½–25cm (9–10in) tall and their small flowers have the varying forms of singles, spoons and quills in a multitude of colours ranging from white and cream to pink and red. At the time of writing, there are several cultivars available to amateurs from Woolman's nursery, with the attractive names of 'Mary Poppins', 'Thumberlina', 'Tara' and 'Charisma'. Culture for these Wye chrysanthemums is similar to that for any other type of chrysanthemum and they are very suitable subjects for both soil and soil-less composts. The latter possibly will give better results, for very small pots are used and moisture is retained much better in the soil-less compost. The only problem is to ensure the necessary twelve hours of darkness from March to early October. Fortunately, plants are small and it is therefore easy to construct a suitable framework using black polythene which can be placed over plants from 19–30 hrs (7.30 pm) to 07–30 (7.30 am) the following morning.

The story behind the breeding of Wye chrysanthemums evolves from a small, insignificant plant which had been used at Wye College for over twenty-five years for house decoration. Originating from seed collected by an English missionary in China and imported privately into this country, the plant became known by the name of 'Chinese Quill'. In 1964, the seedling proved to be self-sterile but the following year seed was produced as a result of a cross with the well-known anemone-centred cultivar 'Long Island Beauty'.

Over several years, further crossings and back-crossings were made to introduce or correct various colours and the medium singles 'Mason's Bronze' and 'Chesswood Beauty' were used for this purpose. The deep red of 'Chesswood Beauty' was particularly strong in some of the seedlings which were displayed at the National Chrysanthemum Society show in November 1972. Although the robust quilled singles are the most productive so far in these seedlings, during the last few years a further break has been established by the production of a range of dwarf pompon seedlings in many colours. Further breakthroughs in form can be expected as some of the old Japanese cultivars, including brush types, have now been introduced by Wye College for further experiments from which many interesting seedlings may arise.

My own observations on these plants, which are substantiated somewhat by remarks made by Alan Jackson, are that many of the dwarf seedlings are of quilled, spoon and spider forms which for some unaccountable reason are not yet fully accepted in this country. America, Japan and many European countries readily accept the decorative value of what are to me extremely attractive flowers, but somehow in this country growers have yet to be educated in this direction. Eventually we may get the lead through our National Society. (A fuller, detailed and illustrated account of this most interesting breeding work is contained in an article by Alan Jackson in the January 1971 *Journal of the Royal Horticultural Society.*)

Bonsai

To most gardeners, the name bonsai immediately conjures up thoughts of aged miniature trees trained into fascinating forms and patterns. Grown with some favour in America but not particularly well-known in this country are bonsai chrysanthemums, which are able to be grown and trained in less than a year into the same forms as the original bonsai. The general culture follows the same pattern as with normal chrysanthemums in regard to the taking of cuttings, stopping, feeding and disbudding; it is the training technique which requires special study.

The first important factor is the choice of cultivars and the best for this purpose are imported from Japan. The main characteristics looked for are a short growth habit but with a vigorous root system; small foliage and long-lasting flowers; and finally the ability to continue to produce new growth on old wood.

Cuttings must be taken very early to allow a long season of growth to enable the main growth to become large enough to give an aged appearance. September or October is the recommended time, although good specimens can still be obtained from a later start in January or February. Treatment of these plants is, in the main, entirely different from that given to other cultivars.

Once rooted, cuttings are initially potted on into clay pots, no larger than 10cm (4in), where they stay until they are almost potbound. A move can then be made to a slightly larger pot. The potting mixture recommended by Ted King, an expert in this field in America, is five parts leaf mould, three parts light clay soil, one part sharp sand, one part fish meal and one part charcoal; this mixture is used for all potting except when over-wintering, when the clay soil is left out.

Cutting back This is the process by which the thickening, tapered trunk is achieved, giving the desired aged appearance. As soon as cuttings are well-established and the plant is about 15cm (6in) in length, the stem is cut back 1½cm (½in) every few days until only 1½cm (½in) of the stem remains. By this time, new shoots will have started to grow from the stem almost at ground level and it is one of these shoots which is retained and grown on according to the style required for the stem. Any unwanted shoots which may develop should be rubbed out.

Pinching or stopping This is the basic means whereby a bonsai grower obtains reduction in the size of plant and proper placement of branches. Once the first stopping has been made around mid-March to mid-April, side-shoots develop and these are retained or removed according to pattern. Further stoppings are made at intervals of about three to four weeks to continue the dwarfing and training process.

Training As soon as lateral growths reach $7\frac{1}{2}$–10cm (3–4in), usually in early April or May, training is started using copper wire to guide growth into the shape and design wanted. Additional assistance is given by small weights hung on developing branches and wire hooks inserted into the soil and used to bring the branches down. Pinching or stopping is again practised to continue the desired growth training and shortening of the trunk and main branches.

Leaf training During spring and early summer, larger leaves are removed from the plant to avoid too much shade being given to the developing branches; these, if shaded too much, will become elongated, a very undesirable characteristic if good bonsai formation is to be achieved.

Disbudding Terminal bud clusters when they appear are gradually restricted down to one main bud in each case, a spare bud being left until the last possible moment to be used only if the main bud is damaged. The object must be to obtain blooms well spaced out over the entire plant.

Exposing roots The exposing of the root system is an important feature of all bonsai plants, and chrysanthemums are no exception. If the plant is first potted on a raised mound, it will not be difficult to expose the main larger roots by watering. The smaller hair roots are then gradually removed until only the large roots remain.

Feeding During the spring and summer, the plants in their very small pots must depend on nutrition given to them with the extensive watering required. A weak liquid feed given every seven to ten days should help to give the plant all the food it needs. It is, however, advisable to stop feeding once the flower buds show colour and for about seven days following repotting or stopping.

At the present time bonsai chrysanthemums are rarely seen in England but, like spiders, quilled and spoon types, they are catered for very extensively in Japan and America. The Americans have special classes for the various types and forms which are a great feature of their shows. It is to be hoped that gradually they will obtain a following in Britain. I am indebted to Ted King of King's Chrysanthemum Nursery, California, for information and help given towards this brief passage on bonsai chrysanthemums.

The names of suitable bonsai cultivars are worth including for their descriptive qualities alone, although I should not like to try and pronounce them.

DWARF CULTIVARS

Hokuto No Aki	Bronze single
Hokuzan No Hakari	White single
Benikagami	Red single
Shinkawe No Hikari	Lavender pink anemone
Shiro Futaye	Yellow single

LARGER CULTIVARS (for cascade or large upright growth)

Attu	Yellow anemone
Ho Syu	Yellow anemone
Koshi No Yuki	White anemone
Kokinran	Red and gold single
Maiko	Rose lavender anemone
Sen Sin	White single

11 *Pests and Diseases*

I am always reluctant to place too much emphasis on the troubles which may beset a prospective chrysanthemum grower, believing that a long list of pests and diseases will deter rather than encourage the production of good chrysanthemums. I should be failing in my duty on this rather sombre subject if I did not give adequate advice which, if followed, will help prevent severe attacks of the most common troubles or at least control them to such a degree that good plants and blooms will still be obtained. It is rather ironical that the celebrated J. H. Goddard, when writing on this same topic in 1951, stated that, unlike tomatoes, chrysanthemums are immune from trouble by way of disease, though there are a number of pests which can cause a lot of concern.

While the pests are still with us in these modern times, in spite of the knowledge and methods of prevention that we now have, twenty-five years after that statement was written we also have more trouble than ever from diseases. In common with modern medical knowledge, this is partly due to the fact that we are now able to diagnose disease more accurately so it is a question of research paying dividends. The answer surely is directly connected with developments that have taken place during the years in the search for new cultivars. Cross-breeding, gamma radiation and probably many other methods have been practised to such an extent that, inevitably, the thoroughbreds of the show bench, unlike the mongrel, do not have inborn resistance to diseases which have probably always been present in embryo.

The subject of pests and diseases should be looked at in its proper perspective, otherwise the slightest discoloration of foliage will be attributed to eelworm while one damaged floret will be considered to be due to a hoard of earwigs. This possibly will appear to be an exaggerated view to many experienced growers, but beginners do tend to think in this way. I recall one occasion when a chrysanthemum grower called me to his plot to seek advice on an attack of verticillium wilt. The only ailment found turned out to be nothing worse than plants wilting because they badly needed a good watering. I have deliberately dealt with this attitude of mind at some length because, although care and attention must always be lavished on our plants, we should not become hypochondriacs about them, and the more obvious reasons should be investigated before an attack of disease is suspected. There is a lot which can be accomplished by growers to forestall the onset of attacks from many pests and diseases, so prior to giving the depressing details of these, a mention of a few precautions to take are worth detailing. Untidy weedy gardens, with piles of old rubbish left around, or rotting wooden fences, are the breeding ground for many pests; clear these up and already a big step has been taken towards controlling many troubles. Weeds act as host plants to various pests which attack chrysanthemums; leaf-miner, as described later, will often be seen on the common ground-sel. Hedges encourage caterpillars, and earwigs shelter under almost anything during the hours of daylight. Unfortunately there is always the risk of an infiltration of pests from breeding grounds outside the immediate area of your control; a nearby neighbour who lets the garden become a wilderness of weeds is a nuisance to everyone, but even in law there is little that can be done and so it becomes very necessary to turn to the use of chemical control.

Chemical Control

Statements attacking the use of chemicals are made from time to time by those who are genuinely interested in environmental problems, and often such publicity leads to the banning of such products as DDT; but while such chemicals may be dangerous when used indiscriminately as drenching sprays from aircraft or large mechanical sprayers used by professional nurserymen and farmers, there is little evidence to show that the amateur in his garden is causing any problems. However, it is always advisable to treat chemical control with great respect, wearing rubber gloves and protective clothing when recommended and above all following the maker's directions to the letter. Failure to do this can lead to serious side-effects, particularly with insecticides based on the organo-phosphorus group.

Basically, insecticides are divided into three main groups for their effectiveness: contact insecticides, which kill pests when they are touched by the insecticides; stomach poisons, whereby chemical material is eaten by the insect; and finally systemic poisoning, where the plant absorbs the chemical into its sap stream either from a spray over the foliage or when watered in at its roots. This latter form of control is very much to the forefront at the present time, as it is effective against sucking insects and has the advantage of remaining very potent for several weeks from one application.

The method of application varies between sprays or dusts for use in the open air and smokes, sprays or dusts indoors, in that order of priority.

It would be relatively easy to control all pests and diseases if there was one all-purpose spray, but this is not the case and so a routine must be adhered to right from the small cutting stage to the large mature plant. Miss out at any stage of growth and before you can look round there is an infestation which will be difficult to eradicate once established.

Many pests have become immune to individual chemicals in the process of survival, so that a change of material used is necessary. My own programme is to spray once every 10–14 days during the early part of the season, using a different kind of spray at each application. I rotate with Malathion, Sybol and Pirimor, but once plants are well established in the open ground or final pots, the systemic Metasystox is used. Any gardener not wishing to use Metasystox is advised to continue the rotation spraying as already detailed.

This spraying is supplemented by dusting powder on the ground around plants, to be renewed after rain; and in addition, with lates, smoke pellets or cones are used once plants have been housed in the greenhouse.

Pests

APHIDS

Aphids are possibly the greatest source of nuisance and under this heading are included greenfly, blackfly and small flies of almost any colour. These are sap-sucking insects, mostly clustered at the end of the stems, although if allowed to they will also build up large colonies on the underside of leaves.

From the time that the stool begins to throw new growths, even before cuttings are taken early in the year, routine spraying must be applied right up to the lifting of the stool or cutting down the plant in the case of lates. Although these aphids can build up into colonies quickly, if a weekly spray is given, or a monthly watering-over with a systemic insecticide, aphids are one of the easiest pests to control. The BHC compounds Sybol, Malathion and Pirimor are all excellent insecticides to use in this control; there are, however, many more products which are equally good. The most difficult control of aphids is when blooms become infested. Unfortunately such infestations are seldom noticed until they have reached severe proportions; if blooms in such a condition were exhibited at a show they would have very little chance of being considered for an award. It is almost impossible to clear an infestation of blooms by spraying, as the insecticide does not penetrate sufficiently into the bloom, but all is not lost as, if blooms are needed for exhibition, they can be washed. It is suggested that experience of this operation is first obtained by using blooms which are not required for showing.

For this purpose, three clean containers are needed—polythene buckets are ideal—and these are filled with insecticide, weak detergent or liquid soap, and clean water, respectively. The bloom is first immersed, upside down, in the insecticide and then, holding it at the end of the stem, it is moved gently up and down several times with a plunging motion. This should ensure complete penetration throughout the bloom and, what is more important, thoroughly saturate any aphids present. After this immersion, the bloom is lifted out and surplus insecticide is carefully shaken out; it is then stood in a vase of water for a couple of hours so that the insecticide can take effect.

The same operation is repeated in the container of detergent or soap. This helps to clean out any dead bodies and excretion present from the occupation by aphids. Finally, a third rinse in the container of cold water is given, and the vase of cleaned blooms is then stood in fresh air, away from any sun, until completely dry. This action will clean all but the worst-affected blooms and can even be used on singles, although extreme care has to be taken not to damage their florets which are far more susceptible to damage than the more conventional double blooms.

It is to be admitted that, once dry, the bloom will probably require some dressing and coaxing of misplaced florets into place, but if this means that an exhibit can be staged then the time spent will have been worthwhile.

There is another very strong reason why control of aphids is vital and they should be prevented at all costs from infesting plants. They are sap-sucking insects, and consequently can readily transfer virus infections from infected plants to clean stock as they move around.

LEAF-MINER

This extremely troublesome pest of the chrysanthemum is a perfect example of why control should be practised before damage is seen. The mature insect is a fly which is very rarely visible but which punctures the outer skin of foliage to lay its eggs. When hatched, the larvae develop by feeding on the leaf's tissue. Leaf-miner maggots can be clearly seen in their tunnels, which cause distinctive white wavy lines as leaf tissue between the two outer surfaces is eaten. If an attack is only slight the maggot can easily be pinched out, but owing to the difficulty of insecticide penetrating through the outer skin of the leaf, chemical control must be concentrated in trying to prevent and deter the fly from laying eggs, rather than killing larvae. BHC, Malathion or Pirimor will again help to control an attack by the fly itself, but once maggots appear in the leaf, a systemic insecticide such as Metasystox is more effective as this works through the sap stream.

I am still of the opinion that, old as it may be, spraying with weak soot water or a weak solution of Jeyes fluid is one of the best means of keeping the fly at bay; in most seasons the vulnerable period is during late May and early June.

CAPSIDS

Green in colour and about the size of a housefly, the capsid moves extremely quickly when disturbed. Another sap-sucking insect, it feeds by puncturing leaves and stems and attacks stems just below buds causing them to heel over as the wound in this thin outer skin of the stem heals up and is drawn together. The buds themselves also suffer from this pest and the results of attacks can be seen as they open, for a segment of the bloom will have florets which do not develop properly.

For complete control, the first step must be to eradicate all weeds as these act as breeding grounds for this pest as well as cover for hibernation during winter months. Here again the difficulty will probably be the inability to keep neighbouring gardens clear of weeds. Control is by means of BHC, Malathion, Pirimor and Metasystox but, because of the pests' swiftness of movement, every part of the plant, including the underside of leaves, must be given a thorough soaking. This saturation of the plants must be done as quickly as possible in the hopes of catching this pest.

FROGHOPPERS

Slightly smaller than the capsid and brown in colour, these jump when disturbed and, in the adult stage, cause damage very similar to capsids. If you are very agile it is possible to hand-catch this pest, but most growers will find it is a little too quick for them. Unlike the capsid, there is an additional time when this pest causes damage. In the spring or early summer, the larvae are surrounded by froth, more commonly known as cuckoo-spit. Because the froth is caused by extracting sap from the plant, damage is also caused by growth being hindered. However, at this immobile stage, the froghopper larva is much more vulnerable, and a vigorous spraying with BHC or Malathion will destroy the froth and leave the larva an easy target. In the adult stage, chemical control is similar to that recommended against capsids.

CATERPILLARS

There are many species of moth responsible for caterpillars which can do a tremendous amount of damage in a very short time. While foliage is sometimes eaten, the worst effects are seen when florets of a developing bloom are chewed. On a small scale, hand-picking is possible but ultimately it is once more a question of spraying to gain any real measure of control; DDT was a splendid chemical for use against caterpillars, but since it has been banned by government order, suitable substitutes have had to be found. Fentro, the brand name for an insecticide containing Fenitrothion, is used for chemical control.

EARWIGS

This common pest, which most growers will be familiar with, attacks both foliage and florets. It is in developing blooms that the devastating effects are seen, unless quick control is administered. The tell-tale signs of earwig damage are large holes chewed out of florets, but you will seldom see an earwig around during daylight as they much prefer to hibernate then, coming out during the night. This pest is certainly one where prevention is better than cure and any rubbish, bricks, stones or pieces of wood will encourage earwigs, as anything which affords cover helps to supply their daytime hiding places. The first rule obviously, is to have utmost cleanliness, but even this may not be sufficient. A second hiding place is in the open ends of bamboo canes supporting plants; a squirt of paraffin from an oilcan will soon kill any earwig lurking there.

Probably the best control of all is to smear a band of vaseline round the stems, just below developing buds; it must also be remembered to smear supporting canes and ensure that it is not possible for this pest to bridge the defences.

Chemical control by spraying with Fentro is again the order of the day, but as earwigs also hide in the ground or travel along it from one plant to another, a periodical dusting around the base of plants with BHC powder is also helpful.

THRIPS

Very minute, small-winged insects, black in colour but so small they can hardly be seen, these mainly damage the chrysanthemum bloom, either as a result of attack in the bud stage or as the blooms develop. A sap-sucking insect, the thrip causes discoloration, which is best described as flecking on the top of the bloom, although thrips most frequently attack and damage flowers of a lighter colour. Damage is more noticeable on the darker colours, especially with a red cultivar, when the white small markings are seen dotted over the florets. Early Red Cloak is a cultivar that often suffers from thrip damage in this way.

This I consider to be one of the most difficult pests to control. Sprayed-on BHC or Malathion are the best insecticides to use, but in no circumstances must you spray open blooms in sunlight. If spraying must be done during daytime, choose a cloudy day; but for preference, late evening is the ideal time for spraying outdoor-flowering cultivars. Greenhouse chrysanthemums can be controlled with BHC or nicotine smokes, but the same rule of not setting off smokes during daytime still applies.

EELWORMS

Eelworms are invisible to the naked eye but the symptoms of their presence, once known, are very easy to distinguish. Starting from the base of the plant and gradually working upwards, in a film of water, eelworms enter the leaves through their very small breathing holes; as the leaf tissue is eaten, dead patches show up as dark brown stains which subsequently turn black. The dead areas first show as triangular or wedge-shaped marks bounded by the thick veins of the leaf and it is this definite triangular formation which is peculiar to eelworm damage. It must not be confused with other discoloration which can be caused by cold or frosts, bruising the leaves by high winds, or by over-feeding.

Chemical control is obtained by nurserymen with Parathion; although this is not sold by horticultural sundriesmen to amateurs and indeed is not recommended by me, many gardeners manage to obtain a supply of Parathion, usually through friends in the trade. This chemical must be treated with great respect and used with caution, taking care not to inhale or allow any of the mist from the spray to drift on to bare skin. The recommendations of suppliers which are always printed on containers must be followed exactly, if you do obtain this chemical. I do admit to using Parathion, but in the safest way I possibly can: not for me a fine spray which may blow back but after lifting and boxing up the stools of earlies and cutting down lates, all the plants are watered over with the Parathion mixture with a fine-rosed can. This kills any eelworms which may be present. Parathion is watered over the plot and once again a fine-rosed can is used; this operation takes place immediately after digging is finished. The third and last application to help control this pest is to repeat the watering over the whole plot, including plants, after planting out has been completed; or when plants have been placed into their larger pots during May.

A further method of eelworm control, although safer to use, is a little more difficult for amateurs because accurate temperature control is necessary. Warm water treatment is used regularly by nurserymen. Amateurs who may possibly have valuable stock of cultivars no longer in commerce can also attempt this, but a very accurate thermometer is essential. The treatment is administered as soon as possible after plants have become dormant. After washing off all the old soil, the stools are immersed for five minutes in water at a temperature of 46°C (115°F) and then plunged immediately into cold water. After removal, the stools are allowed to drain thoroughly and then planted into boxes of fresh compost. Some cultivars do not take kindly to hot water treatment and may be shy of throwing cuttings but few though the cuttings may be, they should at least be free of eelworm. The whole secret of success with hot water treatment is the maintaining of a constant temperature. If the given temperature is exceeded stools may be killed, while a lower temperature may not destroy all of the eelworms.

TERMINAL GALL FLY

Answering to the name of *Paroxyma niscella*, this pest has steadily become more troublesome to chrysanthemums. The symptoms are easy to distinguish: growing tips of either the main stem or breaks, which develop after stopping, swell and give a gouty appearance to the stem. If this swelling is cut open, three or four grubs, usually white in colour, will be found, having developed from the larvae of the fly. All that can be done is to cut back to the next pair of healthy leaves in an attempt to encourage further side-shoots to develop from the leaf axils. If this happens after the normal stopping has been given, it will in effect be the equivalent of a second stop, so size of blooms and flowering time for show purposes is likely to suffer.

Chemical control already given for aphids and other pests should act as a deterent to the fly itself, but once the growing tips have gone blind there is little else that can be done other than the action already described.

SLUGS AND SNAILS

Of these two pests, both of which are too common to describe, slugs cause the greatest nuisance to plants, especially in the very young stage after planting out early-flowering chrysanthemums in the open ground. The small black keel slugs quickly eat through stems and foliage when they are in the young succulent stage but if a few slug pellets, based on a Metaldehyde bait, are sprinkled around each plant immediately after planting, there should not be too much trouble.

WIREWORMS

This, the main soil pest you are likely to come across in the course of ground preparation, is fortunately very easy to identify and, due to its slow, almost undetectable movement, can be readily eliminated. It is more prevalent on new meadow land than in a cultivated garden, where our friends the bird population keep it at bay.

Wireworms are small, worm-like creatures about 2½cm (1in) long, orange in colour, looking very much like pieces of electric bell flex. They attack the stem of the plant just below ground level and can cause the collapse of a plant with a severe infestation. As digging proceeds, any of these which are found should be snapped in two, and a dusting of gamma BHC powder into the top spit should give control. Owing to the life cycle of this pest, it takes about three years to rid the ground of it completely, but once cleared, there should be no further trouble.

BIRDS

Although not looked upon as a pest, as they do help in controlling many other pests in their search for food, birds can be very destructive to young plants in cold frames when hardening-off is in process and immediately following planting out, or potting-on in the case of lates. I do not think for one moment that the nipping out of the growing tips is anything other than destructiveness, or perhaps looking for aphids. As far as my garden is concerned, it cannot possibly be in search of moisture as ample supplies of water are provided all the year round. If protection is not given, sparrows and members of the tit family will attack plants before you can look round. Whether these are planted or just standing out in pots, black tacking cotton should be wound around supporting vanes at various levels in a zig-zag fashion. As a great lover of birds I deplore the advice often given, even in official publications of the chrysanthemum movement, to use terylene. Only tacking cotton should be used: if a bird flies into the cotton it will snap very quickly and will not hurt the bird. Terylene or nylon will certainly not snap and birds can easily become cruelly snared and trapped in this condition all day unless noticed, causing terrible injuries to their very frail wings and legs.

Diseases

The control of disease is often more difficult than keeping pests at bay because of difficulty in identification. It is also true that disease is sometimes thought to be present when in fact symptoms are the result of over-feeding, nutritional deficiencies, low temperatures or other causes, all of which can cause discoloration in foliage at certain times in the year. Generally the uninitiated think about virus troubles far too much. It must not be denied that viruses of all descriptions do exist, and in some instances they are quite common, but often the exaggerated writings of self-styled experts tend to put this out of all proportion. If a disease is identified, the problem, unlike pests which are comparatively easy to kill, is the eradication of that particular disease. Many diseases are so persistent that the only effective means of control is to cease growing chrysanthemums in the affected area for several years. This is not easy for gardeners with small gardens; to rotate a chrysanthemum plot means a severe restriction on the number of plants which can be grown. In consequence, we all tend to keep growing on the same plot but this can still be successful to a very high degree provided that the ruthless destruction of any plant which is suspect in the slightest degree is carried out. I have been growing chrysanthemums intensively on the same plot in my suburban garden for twenty-five years, and only destroy on average ten plants due to suspected disease out of 400 in any one year. This is undoubtedly due to careful selection of stock plants; also absolute attention to cleanliness and, whenever necessary, destroying suspect plants immediately, removing as much of the surrounding soil as is possible, and watering the hole that is left with a strong solution of Jeyes fluid. Unfortunately, even with all these precautions, attacks of certain common diseases of chrysanthemums are possible, so it is therefore as well to identify the most common disease symptoms which are likely to attack plants.

VERTICILLIUM WILT

Caused by a fungus, this disease is quite common and, while some cultivars suffer very severely, others seem to be quite immune. The fungus first enters the roots of plants and travels slowly up the stem. During early stages of vegetative growth, the rate of plant growth is much faster than the speed at which the fungus travels, so nothing unduly odd is noticed; with formation of the bud, stems cease to grow but the fungus travels on. In a short while the sap flow is affected and this leads to wilting of the plant. An unusual feature of verticillium wilt is that it does not always affect every stem of the plant; there can be wilting in one or two stems while the remainder of the plant grows normally. This disease is known to penetrate several feet down into the soil so the only complete cure is to grow elsewhere for several years.

It is possible by sterilization of soil to overcome this disease sufficiently to carry on growing, but once ground is affected, sterilization must be applied each year to keep the top two spits clean and avoid reinfection. Basimid, a soil sterilizer containing Dazomet, is used for this purpose. It is applied as soon as possible at the end of a growing season as its effectiveness is obtained by generating a gas and this can only happen if the soil is still warm. Another helpful agent is Jeyes fluid; apart from watering into the hole left when removing a suspect plant, if a strong solution is also watered over the plot when digging proceeds, a certain amount of control is effected.

VIRUS DISEASES

There are many possible troubles which can be attributed to known or unknown viruses, but it must once more be emphasized that, because something is not quite right with a plant, it should not immediately be assumed that virus contamination is present. There are certain characteristics which do indicate virus infection and these can be clearly defined.
1 Stunted growth with small foliage having a blistered appearance. Undersized flowers with poor colour.
2 Mottled colouring of foliage, again with small flowers.
3 Small flowers which are not typical of the cultivar and with their colour often flecked.
4 Distorted flowers which are also undersized.
Any plant showing these symptoms should be pulled up and burned immediately. On no account use it for propagation purposes. This rogueing of stock is the most essential part of disease control. To this end, whenever plants are being lifted at the end of the season, it is foolish to lift a plant not previously marked as having given good results; a slightly inferior bloom, whether it be in colour, form or size, can always be the beginning of possible virus infection. I do not propose to detail any specific viruses, as visible signs can be confusing; it is sufficient to know the indications as already given. The names Aspermy virus, Stunt virus, mosaic, cucumber virus and tomato spotted wilt all sound particularly hideous, but to most gardeners the knowledge of the names is all that is required—it is the visible signs which are important. Apart from destruction, the only other action recommended is covered by the spraying programme given for controlling pests as, apart from soil infection, sap-sucking insects can transmit disease very rapidly from one plant to another.

CROWN GALL

This disease, also known as leafy gall, causes all growths around the main stem to form clusters of malformed shoots which never develop properly. The shoots look similar in appearance to a cauliflower as they appear just above the soil level. If the cultivar is one which you wish to keep, as the disease is in the soil, any normal shoots which arise from the stool can be used as cuttings, but it must be appreciated that there is an element of risk that these cuttings may still carry the disease, so a careful watch must be kept on any plant propagated in this way.

MILDEW

The chief chrysanthemum disease, this can be identified immediately without any doubt. A floury film develops on foliage and is first seen on the older lower leaves with outdoor plants. It does not usually manifest itself until late in the season and, apart from being unsightly, should not cause much worry.

With late greenhouse cultivars, it affects lower foliage while plants are still standing outside, but it is after housing that mildew can gain a very firm hold unless adequate ventilation is given. Removing all lower foliage below a point where stems formed after stopping helps to give a greater circulation of air. Spraying with Karathane or a sulphur-based fungicide immediately before housing, followed by a Karathane smoke in the greenhouse, will help check this unsightly disease.

DAMPING OFF

A fungus infection, imported in soil used for rooting, this is primarily a disease which affects young cuttings. It shows as a brown ring that rots at soil level; cuttings then collapse and heel over. Sterilized compost, if used, should avoid any attacks; but if close conditions are allowed in a small propagator with little or no ventilation, damping off can still wipe out a whole batch of cuttings. Watering prepared trays of compost to be used for propagation with Cheshunt compound will greatly assist in stopping any attacks. On no account should ordinary garden soil be used completely or partially as a rooting medium, as the spores of this fungus disease will most certainly be present.

ROOT AND STEM ROT

Signs of this disease, usually referred to as phoma root rot, are difficult to detect in the early stages but stunted plants with a yellowing
of the lower leaves and some cracking of the main stem, leading to
wilting in a similar manner to that experienced with verticillium
wilt, may be possible indications; there is, however, fortunately, one
definite means of identification in the case of root rot. If a suspect
plant is dug up, its root system will be poor but there will also be a
distinct dark pink colouring to the roots.

There is no effective control other than giving the plot a rest from
chrysanthemum growing. If this cannot be given and the infection
has not been too severe, a weekly drench with a dithane-based fungicide the following season may give protection and enable cultivation
to continue.

BOTRYTIS

A fungus disease, this is likely to attack young cuttings and mature
blooms in the greenhouse. In both cases the chief enemy is overcrowding, lack of ventilation, high humidity and too much heat. Heat
should only be used to assist the movement of air, by leaving a top
ventilator slightly open so that warm air will rise and, as it escapes,
fresh air is pulled in at the bottom to complete the circulation. The
rooting material affected by this disease should be carefully removed
to prevent any of the active spores infecting healthy cuttings or
blooms. Chemical control in blooms can be obtained by spraying
opening buds with Captan, but I prefer to maintain a buoyant
atmosphere and prevent attack of disease in this way. Although
mostly connected with greenhouse cultivation, attacks can also be
experienced with outdoor cultivars; prevention here is likely to be
achieved if plants are kept growing with reasonably ripe wood; the
use of high-nitrogenous fertilizer will need to be watched fairly
carefully.

PETAL BLIGHT

This disease is quite common and although it can attack both
foliage and flowers it is on the flowers that it is particularly damaging.
The symptoms first appear as small pinkish spots on florets which

then join up with one another as they become areas of wetness that eventually turn brown. The disease is primarily caused by the atmosphere; if persistently wet, blooms out of doors can be affected. Under glass, if the air is not kept reasonably dry and well ventilated, the disease will once more soon become troublesome. Control is mostly on the lines of prevention being better than cure by using chemical control. Captan or Zineb sprays or dusts will greatly assist in keeping this disease at bay in the open while the same chemicals allied to the judicious use of heat and ventilation will look after blooms in greenhouses.

III   Prize-winning multi-vase exhibit at the Surrey Chrysanthemum Show.

12 *Exhibiting*

Once the art of growing top-class blooms for garden and home decoration has been mastered, it is only a short step further to becoming involved in exhibiting. I could well have included exhibiting in the previous section on diseases; once the show bug has bitten, there is really no cure. Medicine prescribed by a doctor will not help. Yet this fanatical devotion to the production of blooms as near perfect as possible has its compensations. Although many friendships are made from sharing this common creative interest, I would place the relief from monotony of everyday existence even higher. It has been said on many occasions that any form of gardening soon brings all its devotees up to the same level, and in no other sphere is this more aptly demonstrated than in chrysanthemum exhibiting; but what is it all about?

It will help a great deal if we first note the aim, as formulated by the National Chrysanthemum Society, towards which all exhibitors strive: 'The main object of a chrysanthemum show is to encourage the growing of chrysanthemums of the highest possible quality.' The various virtues which constitute this quality are discussed more fully in the next chapter on judging.

It is one thing to grow good blooms, but quite another to show them to the best possible advantage. Many a good exhibit, and with it eight or nine months of hard work, has been ruined because of a slight mistake in the preparation for a show.

Planning

Detailed plans, allowing for some adjustment, will help any exhibitor to reach the top flight. Much of this planning will be completed before plants have been set out in the garden or potted into final pots, but no successful exhibitor has ever achieved results in a haphazard way. Luck, quite naturally, plays its part, and this is most likely to affect obtaining blooms on time; it will not rectify neglect in any phase of the cultural programme.

Everything depends upon the target that is set by an individual, in conjunction with the plants grown. To the exhibitor growing 100 plants, five or six entries in single-vase classes will be difficult enough to stage. Similarly a single-handed grower limited to 350 plants attempting to enter a nine-vase class at a national show will be at an obvious disadvantage against two people, whether husband and wife, brothers, sisters or just friends growing 1,000 plants, so results gained on the show bench do not necessarily place exhibitors in order of merit as far as experience is concerned.

Having decided on the particular show or shows to be entered, schedules must be obtained well before the show and a detailed study made of classes to be entered. While show secretaries will not want too many spare entries, it is now an accepted practice to permutate entries to some degree to cover blooms that are actually available; however, a cancellation should be made before the day of the show to avoid unnecessary allocation of space, always a headache for the hard-worked show secretary and his committee.

As the day of the show rapidly approaches, a great deal of time will no doubt be spent walking around blooms, mentally allocating them to the various classes that it is hoped to enter. The list will probably change two or three times a day until the time comes to select and cut blooms.

Cutting Blooms

First I must emphasize the need to cut blooms early. Too many growers suffer from the mistaken belief that they only need cut the day before a show, whereas to ensure that blooms are fully charged with water, cutting must take place at least two or three days before they are needed. Apart from taking up water, the bloom itself increases in size. One golden rule must be followed when cutting: always take the water to the blooms using deep containers. Initially the length of stem should be cut, so that the total length, including the bloom, is approximately 60cm (24in). This allows ample length for stems to be cut when blooms are being staged. After cutting, the end of the stem is slightly bruised or split with either a hammer or a wooden mallet before plunging into a container of water. Many gardeners do not fully appreciate why the stem is crushed: by doing this, a greater area of the soft inner core of the stem is exposed to water and there is consequently less likelihood of an air-lock forming in the stem which would prevent water reaching the bloom. If a bloom shows signs of not taking up water, this can sometimes be cured if the bottom of the stem is put into boiling hot water for a few minutes and then plunged into cold water. An alternative method is to slightly char the end of the stem and again plunge immediately into cold water. Once cut, blooms are best stood in a cool, shady place for twenty-four hours to make sure that they do become fully charged with water.

Selecting Blooms

Whenever possible, the number of blooms required for each vase should include at least one spare bloom for a three-bloom vase and two spares for a five-bloom vase; this allows for possible damage between leaving home and staging at the show.

The main points to be looked for when selecting good show blooms are that each vase should contain blooms which are as near duplicates of each other as possible. They should have size without being coarse, form typical of the particular type, freshness and good colour without variation between blooms. This selection of blooms is an integral part of showing; indeed, success must depend on this. It is no good taking to a show blooms which are sub-standard. They are unlikely to be placed, but what is more, to stage inferior blooms will not exactly enhance your reputation as a good grower or exhibitor.

Transporting

The next stage is transporting blooms to the show without damage. Having spent so much time and effort in producing blooms as near perfect as possible, it would be quite foolish to risk all this work at the last minute by not giving adequate protection. The exhibitor who travels great distances usually takes a little more trouble than the showman who just lives around the corner, but whatever the distance, in most cases transport will be by car. An estate wagon is ideal for carrying blooms, but many exhibitors also manage with a large box secured to a luggage rack on the roof of a car. Suitable cases, racks or hurdles must be made to fit available space. It is better to arrange for blooms to be packed in a vertical position, particularly with large exhibition and greenhouse singles because of the size and shape of the blooms. It would be very difficult to pack them horizontally without risking damage. Without doubt, the best system is to make hurdles which slide into slots in the case. With a little ingenuity small containers of water can be fastened to the stems of each bloom, making sure that the blooms will not deteriorate during the journey.

Blooms of smaller compact types, such as early and late incurves, can be packed horizontally if the stems just below blooms are carefully supported with a roll of newspaper or corrugated cardboard; but I would only recommend packing in this way if it is absolutely impossible to use the vertical system. On no account should tissue paper be wrapped around any blooms, as any vibration of the paper in transit, although soft, will chafe the florets to such an extent that blooms will be unshowable.

Staging

On arrival at the show, absolute priority must be given to unpacking blooms and getting them into water as quickly as possible. There will always be friends and other exhibitors prepared to talk, but they must be brushed off diplomatically at this time or incorporated into your unpacking programme and sent to fill vases with water.

Unpacking completed, then by all means have a walk round, a chat with fellow exhibitors and, if possible, a cup of tea to help relieve the tension which builds up: five or ten minutes spent in this way will put you in a much better frame of mind to proceed with staging.

Having cooled down, vase-up blooms approximately to the various classes which have been entered, making sure that they do conform to the schedule; to have NAS, 'not according to schedule', marked on an exhibit is frustrating and very unrewarding. To this end, read the schedule carefully once more. It is most unwise to assume that the schedule will remain the same each year; if there is any doubt about the correct interpretation, the society show secretary or responsible official must be consulted and requested to give a firm decision. It is true that the wording in the schedule should be perfectly clear, but with the best will in the world there is always the likelihood of a small, simple mistake being unnoticed by the show committee.

All is now ready for actual staging and first any damaged or bruised florets must be carefully pulled out. While some dressing of blooms may have been completed at home, the final finish must now be given, but before dealing with the technical aspect of dressing let us first consider this very controversial subject which inevitably leads to arguments both for and against. I must openly admit that I am strongly in favour of dressing, and the reason is simple enough: few cultivars, if any, can be cut straight from the plant and staged without being tidied up in some way. If a rule were to be introduced banning dressing, great difficulty would arise as to where the border-line lay between tidying and dressing, making the judges' job even more difficult than it is now. There are several safeguards which already control the effects of overdressing. First, florets will very soon show signs of bruising if interfered with too much; as dressing cannot be left until the last minute, any bruising will affect the freshness enough to make it most unlikely that the bloom will be considered for an award. Secondly, if a bloom is dressed completely out of character, the penalties involved would again put the exhibit out of the running. The vast majority of judges appear to interpret dressing in a sensible way and the results satisfy most exhibitors, so at present there is no logical reason to introduce additional rules which in practice could not possibly be enforced.

Having completed dressing and removing damaged florets, the preparation of blooms must be carried to further lengths before they can be considered for the show bench.

Incurves must be as globular as possible and often some of the lower florets, or 'skirt' as these are usually called, must be removed to gain this effect. The top of the bloom should be fully closed over by florets in a clasping manner; if it is loose, in all probability a 'daisy eye' will be showing by the time the judges examine it, and this will lead to its being severely downpointed.

Intermediate cultivars must again be globular, though they are much looser and more open in floret formation. They are not expected in many cases to be fully closed over at the top, although if this does happen in certain cultivars it will not lead to any loss of points. A considerable number of intermediates have a small knot of florets in the centre still to develop, but here the chief fault is the 'letter-box' centre. This is when the small centre knot is elongated instead of being round, but this can be slightly rectified if a few of the short florets at each end of the letter-box are carefully plucked out with tweezers to help give the impression of a round centre.

Many reflexed cultivars demand more in the way of dressing than any other types; many florets require turning downwards or must be coaxed into an even position to give a neat appearance. This can be done with the fingers but the most useful tool for this job is a small plastic or bone knitting needle; never use one made of metal. Florets.

can be rolled down using the small knob end of the needle and with a little practice this can be done very quickly. With florets in the centre of the bloom, the slightly longer ones can also be dressed out to leave a knot of unopened florets in the centre about 2cm ($\frac{3}{4}$in) in diameter. A smaller centre will indicate that the bloom is getting past its best, while a larger centre will only be present when the bloom is rather on the young side. Good reflexed form should therefore be a good solid bloom with depth and breadth in equal proportions, while still having a little more development to come in the centre of the bloom. There are a few reflexed cultivars which have spiky florets similar in character to a cactus dahlia, but if this is the true form of a cultivar then the bloom must be accepted and judged in this way.

Large and medium exhibition cultivars, though not divided into various sections, still follow the same rules governing form; and certainly correcting displaced florets is as important as in any other section of the classification.

Singles, as they have very few ray florets, present a problem. There is a distinct limit to the number of florets which can be removed from them. To avoid damage in transit, a stiff circular collar made of cardboard or plastic is fastened on to the stem and carefully slid up so that it makes a small round table on which the florets can rest. The centre disk will often produce small ray florets, and these should be carefully removed as soon as possible while the blooms are still growing on plants to allow the small hole where the floret has been removed a chance to close up without damage.

Dressing and tidying-up completed, there is one final task that has to be done before staging some of the late-flowering sections. The final item of preparation with large or medium exhibition and exhibition incurves in the late-flowering greenhouse cultivars is the addition of wire supports, canes and false foliage. The use of wire rings is only permitted to support blooms of large and medium exhibition cultivars provided the ring does not exceed $7\frac{1}{2}$cm (3in) in diameter, including padding if used, the object being to prevent these very large blooms from loosing the width at the shoulders of the bloom. The ring consists of galvanized wire about 40cm (16in) in length; the wire is bent at one end to form a circle at right angles to the support. After carefully pushing the wire up the stem so that the ring just touches the underneath of florets, two twist-its are used to firmly fasten wire and stem together, so preventing this wire from slipping down again.

Further exceptional treatment is also allowed with large exhibition blooms; because of their size, after cutting, all foliage is removed so that the bloom will obtain maximum possible benefit from the water in its vase. Although foliage is not judged in this section, it is customary to fasten a length of false foliage to the stem, making exhibits look more impressive.

As many of the cultivars in the late exhibition incurve section have weak stems, the support of a cane or wire is allowed, fastened to the stem only. No rings are permitted, in fact with this type of small compact bloom they are simply not necessary. The question of supports to the stem can sometimes cause a little confusion at late shows, and it is as well to be familiar with the relevant parts of the NCS rules. In the classification for exhibition incurves, the rule states that no rings may be used in this section but supports for the stems may be employed. In class 5, intermediate decoratives, the note to the rule advises that where an intermediate cultivar is grown so that it becomes a true incurve, it is preferable to show these blooms in an incurved class; the exhibitor indicates that he wishes it to be judged as an incurve. The confusion is caused by the fact that, normally, intermediate decoratives are not allowed to have a support to their stem; to give one would result in disqualification. But if the exhibitor opts to enter for an incurved class or, in the case of a multi-vase exhibit, wishes the vase to be judged as an incurve, then a support is allowed. This means that in a show, the same cultivar can sometimes be shown in different classes, with and without a stem support, and both will be correct. 'Gold Foil' is a cultivar which is often employed in this manner.

With blooms all prepared, everything is now ready for the final staging and while time will no doubt be at a premium, undue haste leading to careless staging must be avoided at all costs. Large exhibition blooms are normally staged one to a vase and an overall height of approximately 40cm (18in) will enable the bloom to be viewed to its best possible advantage. It is imperative to stage all blooms at the same height in vases, allowing their interchange to obtain the best colour effect; this is most important in multi-vase classes. After cutting each stem to the required length, crush or split the base again to ensure water will still be taken up. Secure the bloom in an upright position, using wads of moist newspaper, and then top with a layer of moss to give a neat finish.

Blooms in other sections are staged either three or five to a vase, and here a height of approximately 52cm (21in) for the centre back bloom will invariably be the best height to stage. Obviously with slightly smaller or larger blooms the height of the exhibit may need some adjustment to gain maximum possible effect.

There are no set rules laid down as to how blooms are to be presented in vases, but the pattern now commonly used at all shows is that with five blooms, three are staged at the back and the remaining two slightly lower in the front to fill the gaps. Three blooms can be placed either two at the back and one in the front or one at the back and two in the front. It is important that sufficient room is left between blooms so that they can be viewed easily; nothing looks worse than blooms pushing into one another.

Once vasing-up is finished, a further check should now be made if time allows to see if any further dressing is necessary; the few florets in the centre of a reflexed bloom, or an odd floret spoiling the globular outline of an incurve, should all be eliminated. In this way an immediate impression is likely to be made on the judge.

If entries in single-vase classes are now stood in the allotted places on the bench, attention can be given to staging multi-vase classes. There is a considerable amount to learn about staging classes for three, six or nine vases in all sections, though large exhibition blooms have their own requirements.

Cultivars used for multi-vase work should be selected to obtain balance right throughout the exhibit. Size is important and, within reason, cultivars of similar size potential should be staged whenever possible. To stage two or three vases of known smaller cultivars in such classes, while not infringing any rules, will tend to make the whole exhibit look unbalanced. Colour range can also be important and here some switching around of vases may be necessary to counteract the colours of the exhibitors on either side. There is a conflict of ideas in this sphere, whereby some exhibitors stage their darker colours and larger blooms towards the centre of the exhibit and work out to the sides, while others believe in having larger blooms at the two sides. The real answer to this question is not to try to keep to any set pattern drawn up at home, but rather to move individual vases in the exhibit when staged until the best effect is obtained. Somehow or other an immediate and pleasing effect needs to be made on the judge; if this is done, when exhibits are similar in many respects, the initial impression given may sway the decision in your favour. Large exhibition blooms at larger shows are entered in three, six, nine, twelve or eighteen bloom classes, one bloom in each vase; staging in such classes plays a most important part, and size, the prime reason for growing this type of bloom, must be very good. To this end, the selection of cultivars grown is of paramount importance if equality over the whole exhibit is to be maintained. Inevitably there is likely to be some last-minute jockeying for position in multi-vase classes with the vases at the sides of an exhibit. All this is quite legitimate, but I would hope it will always be done in a good humoured way. The exhibitor who takes defeat in his stride will live to fight another day but, above all, he will grow in stature from respect gained from his fellow exhibitors. Nothing is worse than a bad loser, but fortunately there are not many of these around.

13 *Judging*

No section on judging would be complete without first studying the various guide-lines which all exhibitors and judges should be attempting to follow. The National Chrysanthemum Society rules for judging sum this up in the one word 'quality', which by dictionary definition is possibly more aptly described as 'degree of excellence'.

There are six main headings to be considered in this context which, if briefly dealt with, will help all chrysanthemum growers to understand those qualifications called for by the judge, who must attempt to size up all of them in his inspection of an exhibit.

Form

Form is probably the most important facet of all chrysanthemums grown for exhibition purposes. It is the approved shape for each particular kind of bloom which was detailed in the chapter on classification. Basically, form is described as incurved, reflexed, intermediate and single, with one slight variation in the United Kingdom; but the farther afield you travel, the more it will be found that spidery, spoon and anemone-centred often play their part and even take precedence. But all variations take their rightful place and must fit into the judge's mind when he is called upon to officiate in judging a particular type of bloom.

Size

Some exhibitors and judges regard size as the be-all and end-all, and this is probably due to the fact that it is the most obvious thing seen; but there is more to it than that. It should always be remembered that size must be compared at all times to the known potential of a particular cultivar. Any bloom reaching its own potential must obviously, as far as size is concerned, be given maximum credit. This means that often a smaller bloom can win against a larger bloom where the cultivars are different. There can be some difficulty when a new cultivar is in its first season of showing, as the potential of a new release cannot always be known; however, most judges, with the experience they have gained over many years, usually manage to make an intelligent assessment which is acceptable. The only danger with size is when this is obtained at the expense of refinement. An incurved bloom, if grown too large, will tend to become loose in formation, while reflexes and intermediates soon show signs of coarseness.

The final concept of size which normally avoids wrong decisions is that a bloom must have width and depth in equal proportions; to have width without depth gives a saucer-like effect, while depth without width gives an exaggerated, elongated appearance.

Freshness

This is another very important point, for the bloom should be at its maximum stage of beauty, neither too young nor too old. Florets should be crisp and undamaged and any blemishes must be down-pointed accordingly. It is not the judge's job to try and distinguish between blooms damaged in transit and errors in cultivation.

One of the first signs of a stale bloom is when its lower florets become slightly soft or the foliage begins to loose its crispness and becomes a little rubbery. Examination underneath a bloom will often reveal damp or damaged florets, while the centres of large exhibition blooms must always be examined carefully as it is here that damping of florets very often occurs.

Colour

The rules for judging define colour as being good colour typical of the cultivar and this is often difficult to decide in badly lit halls or where artificial light is switched on. Although a laborious task, if any doubt arises with colour the vases concerned must be taken to be viewed in daylight if this is humanly possible. Excessive fading can be due to overprotection or old age; in the latter case the florets will also tend to be a little soft, so that it will attract a double penalty as this fault will also offend the rules governing freshness.

Foliage

Except in the case of large exhibition blooms, foliage must also take its rightful place and again it is here that experience tells; some cultivars have small insignificant leaves, while others have large lush leaves. Once more the phrase 'known potential of the cultivar' must come into the assessment, but whatever the cultivar, any signs of pests such as leafminer must be penalized accordingly.

Staging

The final heading, but a very necessary one, is staging. Blooms placed indiscriminately in a vase with no attempt to arrange must obviously be penalized against a properly arranged exhibit. There are no hard and fast rules as to how staging must be done; sufficient to say that blooms should be presented in a neat and tidy fashion, so that they can all be seen to advantage; and in the case of multi-vase exhibits, vases should be staged uniformly, being at the same height when placed on the same level. Having detailed the various headings it must be noted that they are all inter-related to give a general picture and that they are an attempt to convey some form of standardization in judging. Unfortunately, no matter how many rules are made (indeed, the more that are made the more difficult it becomes), inevitably the success of any system is only as good as the individuals trying to interpret it in a logical way. So let us now consider in some detail all the qualifications and attributes so desirable in a judge, though possibly not always attained.

The Judge

The first rule given in the National Chrysanthemum Society's code of judging states that the object of a chrysanthemum show is to encourage growing chrysanthemums of the highest possible quality. It follows, therefore, that a judge should not only have knowledge and considerable experience but also command the highest respect from exhibitors whose blooms he is to judge. Although many of my fellow judges may not agree, I would add a third qualification, which I consider to be of greater importance than any other quality, and that is he must still be a good grower. I have always felt that the best judges throughout the country are those who are still actively engaged in growing blooms of exhibition standard; admittedly many may have ceased to exhibit in their own right, but often their blooms are used in the inter-society multi-vase classes which are so popular at many of the larger shows throughout the country. Only in this way can a judge keep close contact with, and know the full potential of, the large number of cultivars introduced each year; it is far too easy for a judge to linger on after his active growing days are over and accept requests to judge, often given out of sentiment for past services rendered, rather than bowing out gracefully and giving other good young judges a chance.

Having said this, I will now contradict myself to some extent by saying that age does not, of necessity, make a bad judge. Personality, approach to the task in hand and willingness to still learn after years of judging does allow many of our very senior growers to be amongst some of the finest judges in the country.

NECESSARY QUALIFICATIONS

Although the national chrysanthemum judging courses held each year at various venues in different parts of the country go a long way towards improving the standards of judging, no amount of examinations or tests can bring out many of the vital attributes so necessary in producing the real expert; but at least these courses do select the individuals who are most likely to make the grade, given time and experience.

What, then, are these various characteristics which are so necessary and which added together will make a good judge? Probably the first qualification around which all else revolves is knowledge, but this alone does not sufficiently explain the ideal required without further comment. The theory of what a good bloom should be, as gleaned from various National Chrysanthemum Society publications or by attendance at lectures, is certainly very necessary and desirable; but it must be closely allied to the practical knowledge gained over past years as an exhibitor. It is possibly true that every top-class exhibitor must be able to follow a similar procedure to that of a judge when matching his own blooms, staging them and knowing their potential. However, it is a surprising fact that some growers of this calibre can be biased against, or in favour of, certain sections of cultivars to such a degree that they will never succeed as judges.

The question of knowledge can be summed up by quoting an actual example of an occurrence several years ago at an NCS official course. One very young candidate, who had never grown a chrysanthemum in his life, read and absorbed all the theory relating to judging to such an extent that he was able to pass the test with full honours. However, he afterwards admitted to his examiners that his practical experience was non-existent. Because of this, it was realized that theory was not enough and alterations were made in the provisional selection of candidates so that a prospective judge is now vetted first by a panel of experts to ensure that he or she is a suitably experienced and qualified person; only then can the written test be attempted, in conjunction with a final practical test whereby the candidate satisfies a leading judge or judges that he is indeed worthy of being awarded a certificate of competence, by actually judging all the varying types of blooms in the expert's presence.

The training stage does not usually finish here, unless a new judge is happy to restrict himself to the 'small-time' local shows where his skills will not be taxed to the full. It is usual for any new judge wishing to gain further top-class experience to request an invitation from the NCS in order that he may act as a steward to one of the teams of judges at a national show. From this stage he will progress to being a member of a team of three judges and, if his senior colleagues report favourably on his capabilities, he will gradually move on from single-vase classes to multi-vase classes until eventually he will be proficient in any judging. It will be seen from the use of this system that judges are not created overnight. I must stress that the reason for this lengthy training schedule is not to suppress 'new boys', but rather to see that they know their job and can recognize the correct decisions which should be made and the fundamental reasons behind them.

JUDGING COURTESY

The transitional period from showman to judge is not an easy one, as it is not possible to produce stereotyped judges like sausages from a machine. Contrary to the popular belief among exhibitors, judges are human beings, so consideration must be given to additional factors; consequently variation in character and method of eliminating exhibits and interpreting rules will be inevitable, although in the main the final result is usually the same.

A judge, for his part, must realize that personality and manner of approach gives many exhibitors their first impression of a judge. We have all, unfortunately, from time to time met arrogant judges whose attitude is that, having made a choice, they are not prepared to discuss the smallest difference of opinion with the other members of the judging team or, later on, with exhibitors. Such people fortunately, do not usually last very long, but they can do untold damage in a short while. Good-natured discussion, arguing or talking it out must lead to better knowledge and in the process of doing this, the integrity of a judge willing to talk, will soon become known throughout the chrysanthemum fraternity. Even more important, a judge must consider a necessary part of his engagement to be the willingness to stay behind after the show is opened to the public so that answers can be given to the many questions which are bound to arise from both exhibitors and interested viewers. The latter may not always fully agree with the reasons given for decisions made, but they will certainly respect you for taking the trouble to be on hand and furnish explanations; consequently in most cases they will appreciate your point of view.

AT THE SHOW

Having acquired all the necessary knowledge, what advice can be given to the prospective or new judge on the best way to tackle his vital task? First and foremost, never get flustered; and to avoid this at the outset, it is advisable to arrive at the show in plenty of time to meet the show secretary and his organizing committee. As a judge is one of the most important people at the show, a certain amount of social contact is very necessary. Great care must be taken, however, to see that until the hall has been cleared ready for judging, the staging area where blooms are being vased and the exhibition hall itself are avoided at all costs. Conversations with old exhibiting friends must wait until judging has been completed in the interests of the very familiar phrase, 'Justice must be seen to have been done'. Never allow the slightest possibility of any subsequent close decisions being criticized and subjected to accusations of favouritism. The period of waiting can always be well-employed in discussion with fellow judges and studying the schedule. The new judge must never allow himself to become overawed by any well-known personality with whom he may be judging, as every judge has been invited by the society in his own right to express opinions, and not just to be a 'Yes-man'. I personally have a natural tendency to give a running commentary of my decisions out loud as I think when judging, which is always a source of amusement to the stewards who accompany me on my rounds; but most of them say they learn a lot from this.

After the hall has been cleared, a walk round to accustom your eyes to the light and obtain a general impression regarding the standard of the show will complete your preparation for the real task of judging.

I do not propose to comment on all the faults for which a judge will be looking, as most of these were detailed in the chapter on exhibiting, but there are many possible pitfalls which await any judge allowing his concentration to lapse, even for a few seconds.

Although actual interference from a steward must not be encouraged, it is of the utmost importance that he should be brought into the picture and know you will welcome comment when it appears that something has been missed. It is possible, even at a national show, for a vase or exhibit to be completely overlooked, especially if spaces are left in a class by competitors who have not filled an entry, as it is not usual to move exhibits until after completion of the judging. This can prove to be quite embarrassing, so it is essential to impress on your steward at the outset exactly what you require him to do, and in particular to check the number of entries staged in each class, although this does not relieve you of the final responsibility.

Manhandling of blooms must be avoided—it is not necessary to pull a bloom apart to see if there is anything wrong. An exhibitor may want to keep the blooms staged for many reasons, and he will not thank you for unnecessary damage. I well remember a judge, no longer with us, who many years ago was a prominent member of the NCS executive. This was before the introduction of judges' courses, and because of the shortage of judges, he was always fully booked to judge. His favourite trick was to take a very heavy silver pencil, poise it about 15cm (6in) above the centre of an incurved bloom with the rounded part of the pencil pointing downwards, and then to release the pencil suddenly. If the pencil bounced off the bloom it was, in his opinion, a good tight incurve; if it penetrated into the florets, they were considered to be too loose and would seldom be given an award. Obviously such treatment, even in a winning vase, meant bruised blooms, as could be seen towards the close of the show.

Unfortunately there are still a few judges around who, while they may not use this technique, are not as careful as they might be and cause damage by mauling blooms.

SHOWMEN'S TRICKS

While in a reminiscing mood, and to illustrate just how thorough a judge must be, I recall one memorable occasion when a well-known

IV   Charm chrysanthemum: Golden Chalice.

exhibitor, in his keenness to fulfil all his entries at a London national show, calmly created the illusion that some reflexed blooms were not blown in the centre by expertly sticking back the offending central florets. So well was this done that the only way it could be detected was by lightly touching the centre of the bloom with a finger, when the florets would be found to be quite hard. It could not be detected visually and I have encountered this on several occasions since from other exhibitors, so I always use this light finger touch as part of my permanent judging procedure with reflexed blooms; it is probably a point well worth passing on, as in every competitive sphere there will always be someone who will attempt such forms of deception, usually classed as 'fair cheating'. Another breach of the regulations, often deliberately perpetrated, is using a wire ring and padding which exceed the stipulated diameter of 7½cm (3in) to gain a little extra width on the shoulders of a large exhibition bloom. Here again, the difficulty of checking this makes it possibly more prevalent than many growers or judges would care to admit; but if there is any doubt, I would not hesitate to have the suspected bloom out of the vase, after checking for staging, so that it can be turned upside down and properly measured. I would add that this should be done in the presence, not only of a steward, but also of a member of the show committee or an official of the society as a witness.

POINTING SYSTEM FOR JUDGING

It is a fact that an elaborate system of awarding points has been devised by the NCS, supposedly to assist judging, but I do not propose to dwell on this for a very good reason. Few if any judges will ever need to make a decision based on points, as the various degrees of quality laid down are more than enough to arrive at a decision and the points, therefore, are meant only as a guide to their importance. In all my years of judging, I can only remember one occasion when I went through the ritual of awarding points, and this was only used to demonstrate the accuracy of judging without points. On this particular occasion I had assisted with four other well-known judges at a large society show, and a final decision had to be made as to which exhibit was to be awarded the trophy as best exhibit in the show, now usually called the most meritorious exhibit in show. The exhibits under consideration were both multi-vase classes, one for three vases of five large blooms, the other for two vases of five mediums. Four judges voted for the vases of large and one for the mediums, so there really was no argument; but as there was time in hand, two of the judges suggested that, as an exercise, we all point the exhibits and then take an average to arrive at the result. The four judges were proved to be right, even to the satisfaction of the fifth, but personally I would like to see all reference to a pointing system abolished. It tends to be stressed too much to beginners, when practically every experienced judge agrees that it is not necessary in these modern times. Chrysanthemum exhibitors as a whole are now thoroughly conversant with known standards of form, freshness, size, etc, and points are just out-dated.

COMPLETING THE TASK OF JUDGING

Show organizers are a race of optimists where the time required to judge a show is concerned; far too often insufficient time is allowed between the completion of staging and the official time for opening to the public. A good judge will never allow himself to be hurried on this account; if the prescribed time arrives and judging has not been completed, the decision as to whether the public are admitted or not must be the decision of the organizers. The judge should continue unhurriedly and complete the job to his own satisfaction; only then can he go to his lunch with a feeling of achievement.

There have been occasions when I have heard visitors criticizing judging. Whether one is an exhibitor or a visitor to the show, before passing comment a really detailed inspection of the exhibit concerned should be made; there is usually a reason for an apparently good vase not receiving an award: an infestation of aphids may be in one or more of the blooms; faults at the back of the vase or underneath the blooms are not readily seen; and the length of time from judging to viewing must be taken into account. If, after this close examination has been carried out, a mistake still appears to have been made, then register a protest in accordance with the procedure laid down in the schedule. To grumble and do nothing about it is the height of foolishness.

14 *Raising New Cultivars*

New cultivars always command an intense interest from chrysanthemum growers, most of whom buy several new introductions each year. Although it is usually considered that the professional nurseryman is ideally suited to raise and introduce new cultivars, nevertheless there are already many well-known amateur raisers throughout the world and this number could possibly increase.

Most amateurs start by growing chrysanthemums for garden decoration or cut-flowers and gradually, as interest is aroused, many turn to exhibiting. Here, for many growers, the story ends, but there are a few with the necessary patience and determination to embark on raising new cultivars of their own.

I am indebted to George Wilson, a very knowledgeable raiser of new cultivars, for helping me and allowing me to publish some of the following information. My reason for including this chapter in a book intended primarily for amateurs is twofold: apart from information assimilated by knowing how new cultivars are grown from seed, there is always the possibility that sometime one of your plants may throw a new 'sport', and if this happens, at the very least you will have some guide to the treatment which should be given.

Sports

A sport is the term given when describing a change which sometimes occurs in a cultivar; this may relate to colour, shape of the bloom, vigour or habit or growth or the normal date of flowering. Here we are mostly concerned with the first two properties, namely change of colour or form.

The scientific explanation is far too involved—indeed I am not qualified even to attempt such an explanation. I am quite happy to be told by our scientific friends that it is all a question of chromosomes and genes. However, I do understand the implications of the term genetic change or breakdown, which can be either natural or artificially induced by irradiation where, by exposure of the cells of plants to gamma rays, dozens of changes can be made. I am not convinced that artificial interference with nature is a good thing, in fact many of our present troubles, leading to the quick breakdown and deterioration of many modern cultivars, are probably traceable to the use of irradiated stock. I am, however, interested in sports which occur naturally, albeit because of the unstableness of a cultivar, which I expect the scientists will say is no different from an artificially induced change.

This natural sporting can occur at any time, and if it can be fixed then a new cultivar has been created. The most common type of sporting is for one or more stems of a plant to produce blooms entirely different from their parent, colour variation being instantly recognizable. To give examples, from the pink 'Eve Gray' we have had 'Bronze Eve Gray' while 'Margaret Riley' (pale pink) has sported 'Bronze Margaret Riley' and 'White Margaret Riley'. This white sport in its turn has given 'Yellow Margaret Riley' so, as you can see, there is no end to what can happen once sporting has begun. I have deliberately written the name in full each time to pinpoint the fact that, according to regulations governing the naming of chrysanthemums, the name of a new sport should include the whole or part of the name of the parent cultivar from which the sport arose.

If the sport arises with an outdoor plant, the whole plant should first be carefully lifted and potted to make it much easier to handle; lates will of course already be in a pot. All growths, other than the stem or stems producing the sport, are trimmed away to encourage production of side-shoots on these, which are needed to supply suitable material for taking cuttings.

A long, narrow wooden box is now made, about 15cm (6in) deep and a slit is cut in one end about 7½cm (3in) deep and 2½cm (1in) in width. Now half fill the box with John Innes No 1 compost up to the bottom of the gap which has been made. After removing the leaves and watering the pot well, it is laid on one side so that the stem which carried the sporting bloom rests in the notch and lies horizontally on the compost. Another layer of compost about 5cm (2in) deep is added, so that the stem is covered. After watering, a heat of at least 13°C (55°F) must be maintained. Side-shoots will gradually develop from the old leaf axils remaining on the stem and break through the compost in the same manner as basal shoots grow from the stool of a plant. These shoots should be grown on until long enough to be taken as cuttings in the normal way. After rooting, pot on and either plant out the following season or use as a stock plant to produce cuttings which can be taken early the following year. Eventually, when the plant flowers, it will be seen whether or not the sporting has been retained. If it has, then you can be reasonably certain that it has been fixed. At this stage, if the break from the parent is sufficiently pronounced for it to be generally introduced, I would suggest that steps are taken at once to have the cultivar registered and then a commercial grower who will have the means and facilities for its marketing is contacted. The International Committee on Horticulture Nomenclature and Registration has appointed the National Chrysanthemum Society (Great Britain) as the international registration authority for the names of chrysanthemums, so it will be necessary to apply to the secretary of the NCS for details and instructions regarding registering and classifying.

New Cultivars from Seed

As with all forms of breeding, considerable knowledge and experience must be acquired before embarking upon a deliberate chrysanthemum-breeding programme. Each crossing is likely to produce 100–200 seeds, so considerable space is required to grow plants during their first year; you cannot afford to neglect one single seed, as this may be the very one that is a potential winner. Naturally the second and third year of a particular crossing will see a big reduction in the number of plants grown as unsuitable seedlings are discarded, but by this time successive crossings will be under way. It is probable that most amateurs may have to enlist the help of other amateur growers to grow some of the seedlings, because of the space problem.

PREPARATION

Before any crossing can be made, it is necessary to have good clean healthy stock for crossing. Detailed records will have to be kept from the start, as the computations which can be made run into thousands. It has been found that in a considerable number of crossings, best results are obtained when using plants of the same type and colour for the crossing, although nature can in many circumstances achieve quite remarkable results. Generally large-flowering plants are crossed with large, medium with mediums, incurves, reflexes or intermediates all with their own types, and the same system applied to colours. Often it will be found that a first crossing is made and a seedling from this crossing is eventually used to make a second crossing which, if desired, can be back to one of the original parents. The permutations have no limits.

While the predominant factor of a crossing does not follow any firm rules, it usually results in 90 per cent predominance as far as the plant is concerned, though the flower form can vary considerably. This means that if crosses are made large with large, 90 per cent of the progeny will be large, and mediums with mediums will again produce a good percentage of mediums.

Hybridizing for colour does present considerable difficulties in anticipating the outcome, especially when crossing two different colours with one another. If a bronze is crossed with a yellow this will give reds, yellows and intermediate shades of bronze and light bronze, while a white and red cross may give reds and intermediate shades of pink. However, the likelihood of obtaining definite colour changes when cultivars of the same colour are crossed varies very little. Examples of these crossings from experiments made are that when yellow is crossed with yellow, yellow still dominates all the resulting blooms, but when yellow is crossed with white only 40 per cent of the resulting progeny are yellow. White with white gives 90 per cent white, whereas pink with white gives only 12 per cent pink. Similar percentages were obtained with other colours.

Having decided on the parents to be used, after rooting cuttings, plants are grown in boxes or small pots under starvation conditions; this results in small daisy-eyed blooms, as plants endeavour to perpetuate themselves in the belief that they are dying. This enables pollen to be collected easily from the pollen-bearing plant, while the stigmas of receiving plants are exposed, making them easier to pollinate. I would suggest that possibly the best way to start is to concentrate on the early-flowering outdoor cultivars, as too much greenhouse space will be required if late-flowering cultivars are used.

POLLINATING

The process, although the same for all types of blooms, can be most easily understood if it is described for pollinating single cultivars as the central disk florets are readily visible in this most simple form of flower.

The centre of the bloom consists of a small cushion of disk florets which have both male and female organs, while the longer outer ray florets are only female. The ray florets are gradually cut back as

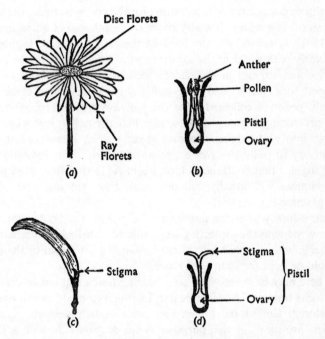

Fig. 9 Anatomy of the chrysanthemum: (*a*) the complete flower, (*b*) disc floret, (*c*) ray floret, (*d*) ray floret cut back. Pollen is transferred from anther to the disc floret (*b*) to the stigma of cut-back floret (*d*).

they develop until the female pistil can be seen, making it easy to apply the pollen.

The two prepared flower heads which are to act as the pollen-bearer and seed-bearer are cut with 30–45cm (12–18in) of stem and after removing foliage are placed in containers with approximately 7½cm (3in) of water in them. The heads are protected against flies and pests, which could upset the crossing programme, with small muslin or paper bags. While waiting for the pollen to ripen, the heads are stood in a warm, dry, airy room or greenhouse at a temperature of 15–17°C (60–65°F); the level of the water must be topped up regularly with water at the same temperature. As soon as the pollen is ripe and stigmas of the chosen seed-bearing head show as a Y-shaped fork, all is ready for pollinating. With a fine camel-hair brush, pollen is collected from the pollen-bearer and transferred to the protruding stigmas, making sure that the pollen is worked well down into each stigma. Because stigmas ripen in succession, it is necessary to pollinate over a period of several days, re-pollinating any stigmas that continue to look fresh. As fertilization takes place, the stigmas will usually collapse, indicating that this part of the programme is complete.

Immediately after the application of pollen, the heads should be re-covered with the protecting bags, suitably labelled or numbered to coincide with a record book note in which every detail of the cross should be kept for future reference.

There may be times when seed-bearing heads will not be ready at the same time as the pollen-bearer, in which case pollen will have to be stored. Collect the pollen and place in tissue paper: cigarette papers are ideal for this purpose. A tin or glass tube with a tight-fitting lid or stopper is now prepared by placing a small amount of silica-gel in the bottom; then, after covering with some cotton wool, place the little sachets of pollen on this and after putting some more cotton wool in the receptacle, tightly seal and place in a cool dark place where the pollen will still be usable up to about ten or twelve days from collection.

HARVESTING SEED

After fertilization, the seed takes approximately eight to twelve weeks to ripen properly. On no account should the seed head be interfered with. Seed will be ready for harvesting when the seed head disintegrates naturally and the protective bag will ensure that no seed is lost.

When ready, the seed husks can be emptied on a sheet of paper and the husks carefully separated from the seed which should then be enveloped, marked with the crossing number and kept in a dry, airy room ready for sowing.

SOWING THE SEED

During February the seed of crossings of both early and late-flowering cultivars is sown in John Innes seedling compost; soil-less compost can be used if preferred. A temperature of 15°C (60°F) should be sufficient, although the time taken for germination can be very erratic, some seedlings appearing after about fourteen to twenty-one days while others can take as long as four to nine weeks; the trays or pots in which the seed is sown should not, therefore, be discarded too quickly. As soon as the first two seedling leaves are formed, seedlings should be pricked out into seed trays containing John Innes No 1 compost. As soon as they are established in the trays, they should be moved into the cold frame and treated from then onwards in the same manner as ordinary cuttings.

TREATMENT OF SEEDLINGS

Treatment of seedlings during their infancy varies according to the whims of individual breeders. In conjunction with the methods described here, it is recommended that, to reduce the normal tendency for almost excessive hybrid vigour in the seedlings, a tip is taken from each seedling and rooted as a normal cutting. This helps to reduce this natural vigour, making it very much easier to assess the potential of the seedling.

Stopping in this first season is carried out on one date for all seedlings, 25 May being a suitable time; any seedlings which are retained can be adjusted in the following season. The number of breaks kept per plant will vary according to the number produced: four to six will be the average, and from this number a reasonable assessment of the bloom will be practicable.

Feeding seedlings is not desirable during the first season, as it is likely to give a distorted idea of the true value of resulting blooms. Provided ground has been well prepared, nothing more in the way of feeding is required.

During the first year it is very rare for disease to be present, though every precaution must still be taken as previously advised when dealing with pests and diseases.

ASSESSMENT

If possible, every seedling germinating should be grown on to give the greatest choice possible when selection is being made. A point which the inexperienced breeder must bear in mind is that the second year of growing is the time to tell whether or not a seedling is worth keeping. During the first season of growth, resulting blooms can be classified under three headings for suitability as exhibition or garden decoration plants: these are, excellent, mediocre and unsuitable. All but the last category should be retained, as often during the second year an excellent bloom will prove to be poor, while a mediocre one, on further trial, may be worth keeping.

When blooms mature, many differing forms will be found ranging from singles and spidery-petalled cultivars to malformed, bi-coloured blooms; but there will certainly be one or two showing promise.

In assessing seedlings, there are several factors that must be considered at the outset. The habit of a plant is often taken very much for granted, but ideally this should be compact, upright and straight in growth. A plant with stems sprawling or bending outwards would need to have an exceptionally good bloom for anyone to buy it. Foliage should be reasonable in size according to the bloom, evenly spaced on the stem and not crawling underneath the bloom. Height does not appear to be of much concern with the raiser of today and this possibly may be due to the availability of the chemical B9 which can be used to dwarf a cultivar artificially. It should not, however, be necessary to resort to chemical control for governing height. Outdoor early-flowering cultivars should not exceed $1\frac{1}{2}$ metres (approx 5ft) as the absolute maximum. To try cultivating plants which grow 2 metres ($6\frac{1}{2}$ft) in height, as is experienced with Pat Amos and sports, leads to many problems. Late-flowering greenhouse cultivars are notoriously tall growers, but the average amateur with a small greenhouse cannot cope very well with heights of $2\frac{1}{4}$–$2\frac{1}{2}$ metres (approx 8–$8\frac{1}{2}$ft). Finally, colour should be very distinct and clear; any loss in the richness of colour as the bloom develops must be frowned upon, while natural bi-coloured cultivars should have the colours clearly defined on each side of the florets.

This, then, is the task facing the would-be breeder of new cultivars; many disappointments will be experienced, but it only takes one good winner to become a household name in the chrysanthemum fraternity.

15 *Chrysanthemums in other Countries*

America

As is to be expected in such a vast continent, dates when cuttings are taken in America and the timing of various tasks allied to good culture differ considerably, although basic methods are similar in nature to those employed in England. However, in the types of blooms grown and shown there is a considerable difference, which all our American friends notice as soon as they visit shows in Britain. Most American society shows make a feature of sprays, spiders, quills, spoons and pot plants such as bonsai and cascades. Floral art and decorative classes are also an integral part of showing, which is attributable to the very active part played by the ladies in all phases of chrysanthemum culture. To a mere Englishman, much of the information contained in the *Bulletin* of the America National Society is quite novel; indeed I would venture, as a member of the Publications Committee of the NCS in this country, to suggest that there are many ideas we could adopt with some success. Society news, reader participation and items of information are far more extensive in America, but it is in the realms of the American society *Show and Judges Handbook No 6* that some of the most fascinating details are set down.

One of the first obvious points is the difference in classification, due to the fact that here in England we have two distinct seasons, namely, early and late-flowering. American classification places the type of bloom in its appropriate class purely on form and not on time of flowering; quite often it is the practice to show both early and late-flowering types at the same show.

The exhibition cultivars introduced from England that we know as earlies are shown in disbudded classes. A few examples taken from a catalogue of King's Chrysanthemums Nursery, California, which imports a great number of British cultivars, illustrates this point. 'Arthur Blythe', 'Duke of Kent' and 'Gigantic' are all classified as section 1, large exhibition, in Britain; yet the American classification is 5-incurve, 8-reflex and 6-reflexing incurve respectively. In the American exhibition incurve section, all classified as section 5, we have 'Betty Wiggins' (Brit. 25A), 'Connie Mayhew' (Brit. 2), 'Crimson Daily Mirror' (Brit. 5A) and 'Maylen' (Brit. 3B).

The decorative section, with an American section 7 classification, contains 'Broadway' (Brit. 24B), 'Goldplate' (Brit. 15A), 'Mary Jefferies' (Brit. 5A), 'Standard' (Brit. 24A) and 'Staybrite' (Brit. 25B). This may all sound very confusing yet, as I write, there has already been a suggestion that a similar system be adopted here in England whereby early and late cultivars can be shown at any time of the year in their appropriate classes. Whether or not this will be accepted remains to be seen.

The remainder of the American classification is mostly connected with sprays and the more exotic types of spoons, quills, spiders, laciniated and brush or thistle-like cultivars.

In some areas (eg west coast) where the introduction of many British cultivars has been made, the British classification is used for this particular type of chrysanthemum.

In colour classification there are yellow, white, purple-pink, bronze-orange, red and other, as opposed to the eleven colours in the British list. One rule I find peculiar is that shades of green are placed in the white class, whereas we classify this as another colour. Generally show organization rules once more show the complete involvement of society members in America by the appointment of a chairman to cover each of the different aspects of a show. While some combination of tasks is determined by the size of the show, generally each of the following categories is the complete responsibility of one individual: general show schedule, entries, classification, judges, hospitality and awards. Larger shows may require additional coverage for such items as publicity and photography. It is as well to note that the various chairmen are appointed early each year, so that they can take full responsibility for all arrangements in their own particular field. While we in Britain might think this is over-planning, the running of the American type of show requires a lot of organization. Frankly, speaking from personal knowledge, the typical British method whereby arrangements usually descend on one or two willing horses, makes it appear that more organization here on these lines might prove to be very welcome, but much would depend on the present-day show secretary and his willingness to delegate various tasks to his co-chairmen. A section about American shows would not be complete without studying one or two definitions which I find quite delightful in the manner of their expression.

An Amateur One who grows chrysanthemums for pleasure and excellence without financial gain (his income from the sale of chrysanthemums does not exceed his cost of cultivation). It is expected and required that no professional or paid labour give aid to your growing, except with the preparation of the soil. This help may only function before cuttings are placed in the ground. One exception is permitted: paid labour may help in the construction of a shelter for the disbud bed.

A Professional A person who makes his living from his knowledge of chrysanthemums, either by writing, lecturing, research, teaching, breeding or selling plant material (wholesale or retail).

Etiquette and Ethics for the Exhibitor Ethics of amateur exhibitors should run as high as they do for any kind of sportsmanship. No one should think of doing anything that would be distasteful or embarassing to the organization and its rules. Etiquette is as important to an exhibitor as it is to a judge. At all times he should be polite, tolerant, helpful and cheerful and can contribute to the success of a show by preparing his entries without aid, confusion, selfishness or aggressiveness.

Ethics in Judging Briefly, the directions laid down are that no judge criticizes the judging of other judges and that he should frequently examine his approach and attitudes. He should have an awareness of his faults and attempt to correct them. By so doing, he will create and maintain a reputation for his integrity.

Etiquette for Judges A judge should be enthusaistic, his manner direct, his decisions firm. His bearing should be dignified, sincere and gracious. Tact and courtesy are essential, particularly where an agreement in judging may call for self-restraint. The judge's voice should be quiet, never loud or argumentative. In a discussion of the relative merits and faults of an exhibit, a judge should be willing to give his decisions and the reasons for them, but at the same time have respect for the differing opinion of another judge. Levity, arrogance, sarcasm and disparaging remarks are violations of good conduct. Negligence, carelessness and evasion of judging duties are violations of standard show practice. As a finale I quote: 'It is customary for a judge to be well groomed, conservatively and carefully dressed in a manner befitting the occasion and the time of day. Judges, as ladies and gentlemen, should wear normal city street attire.'

From this, there would appear to be a great need for us in Britain to issue similar guide-lines in an official publication; many of the directions are only a matter of common sense, but it is the kind of code which, if not followed, should lead to any judge's being withdrawn from official judging lists.

CULTIVATION

It is not possible to lay down any hard and fast dates because of the great climatic variations and latitudes under which plants are grown and blooms mature. It is said that the climate of Texas is similar to that of the homeland of the chrysanthemum species, China. In California, because of warm weather conditions, it is almost impossible to grow good large exhibition blooms without showing an eye. Most of the cultivation here is done in the open garden, protection being given by covers in a similar way to that employed in Britain. Further north, but still on the west coast, nearer to the Canadian border, large exhibition blooms are quite a feature at places like Seattle. It must be appreciated, however, that shows are planned to take place in late October and cuttings are taken accordingly during the period of April to June.

The advice given to American growers is to take cuttings as late as possible according to locality and weather, as late cuttings make shorter growing plants. A glance at a map will quickly convey to any reader that with such great distances north/south and east/west as there are in America, timing must of necessity be much more local than it is in this country, where the distance between Scotland and the south coast is infinitesimal in comparison. Stopping, or 'pinching' to use the American expression, is practised very extensively to obtain timing of blooms, several stoppings sometimes being given.

In controlling pests and diseases, systemic insecticides such as Metasystox and the fungicide Benlate, also systemic, are the chief sprays used. From my own experience of using both of these products in this country, I can vouch for their effectiveness; there does not seem to be any need to fear using Metasystox if reasonable precautions as described by the manufacturers are taken.

The growth retardents B9 and Phosfon are used to control the height of plants far more than we do. Possibly this may be due to the much smaller choice of cultivars compared with those we have.

It is not easy for new British cultivars to be introduced, as very stringent quarantine regulations have to be complied with before a plant is generally released in America. The position in this field is improving, but I cannot imagine that American shows will ever be on the same lines as those in Britain, any more than ours will be modelled on American lines. But just as British exhibition cultivars are being introduced into America, there is certainly room for many of the typical American sprays, quills, spiders and similar cultivars to be introduced to shows in Britain.

Australia

Although, like America, Australia covers a very wide area, serious chrysanthemum growing compared to the United Kingdom is on a very small scale. In consequence specialist supplies are rare, and keen growers have to be 'do it yourself' experts in addition to their growing abilities. Chrysanthemum fertilizers, compost, insecticides and many other necessities according to our standards are often non-existent. Cultivars grown are mostly in the late-flowering section, as British early types, because of their earlier flowering time, do not stand up so well to the intense heat experienced in most of the Australian states at the time of bloom maturity. Tasmania is said to be the most suitable state in Australia for chrysanthemum culture because of slightly lower temperatures. Victoria is considered to be the next best state and it is understandably in these two states that we have two well-known Australian growers, Tas Jones and Bruce Furneaux. Both have visited the mother country and I have been privileged to have had many hours of interesting conversation with them. Bruce, a breeder of some note in Australia, on his return from visiting this country in 1973, took back with him as many of the newer British novelties as was allowed under the regulations, hoping to introduce them in Australia. Here, as with most overseas countries, strict export and import regulations apply and plants are subjected to a very precise quarantine programme. A nurseryman or breeder is only allowed to import into Australia, on licence, 250 plants in twelve months: twelve plants of a cultivar if unrooted cuttings, or six if rooted. Plants are first under sole charge of the Department of Agriculture, Botanical Section, which conducts a series of very rigid tests with particular emphasis on possible diseases. Plants that survive these tests are used for propagation purposes and it is cuttings from these tested plants which are eventually released. It will be realized from this that the importation of new cultivars is not easy.

In Sydney the weather is very humid, and larger blooms give way to spiders, quills and singles, following the Japanese influence in the same manner as on the Pacific coast of America. Queensland and South Australia are somewhat lacking in chrysanthemum growers while Western Australia has a number of excellent growers who manage to cultivate their chrysanthemums under extremely difficult conditions. Seasons are, of course, opposite to ours and during the Western Australian summer it is common to have temperatures of 40°C (104°F) combined with a very high humidity, hardly good chrysanthemum-growing weather. Much of the success in this state is due to the hard-working officials of the Western Australian Society.

Growing methods in Victoria revolve mostly around the late-flowering cultivars which are grown in open ground, cover being given at flowering time. Large exhibition plants are often grown in large tins, simply because large clay pots are difficult to obtain. Cuttings are taken in July for large exhibition cultivars and given a first stop in mid-October; a second stopping in mid-December usually gives buds in early February. Some idea of the temperature range at this time can be gauged from the fact that from the end of September to December it is likely to be 22°C (72°F), while after Christmas, when buds are in the initiation stage, it will be up to 40°C (104°F). At the time blooms mature, humidity is very high, resulting in a great deal of loss in blooms from damping. The effect of these very warm bright days manifests itself in the height of plants, 2–2½ metres (6½–8ft) being quite common. Contrary to the situation in America, the use of growth retardents such as B9 and Phosfon has hardly been explored, but this may be rectified in the near future as more publicity is given to these useful chemicals; the question of availability has still to be resolved.

One item of extreme interest to me when listening to a lecture given by Bruce Furneaux was the details he gave on how crushed polystyrene has been used very successfully to replace sand in mixing potting composts. While there is no apparent need to use this in England, some experiments in this direction might prove worthwhile. It also appears that the art of dressing blooms, at least as far as the state of Victoria is concerned, is not known or practised to any degree. This is borne out by some of the slides seen of mature blooms. While over-dressing is to be avoided, there obviously is a great need for some instruction on dressing to be given; it is a great pity that our countries are so far apart that we cannot easily exchange lecturers and demonstrations on such subjects.

Tas Jones, who has grown chrysanthemums for exhibition in the state of Tasmania for close on forty years, uses the following system of culture which must be of interest to many readers. His methods, in some respects, may seem a little strange compared to ours, but when studied they follow a very logical order and understandably are successful under the very different conditions.

When preparing the ground, because of the need to improve the soil, raised beds are constructed to give plants a depth of good soil sufficient to ensure the necessary root system so vital to producing good blooms. Beds are just over 1 metre in width (approx 3½ft) and are edged with boards 25cm (10in) wide and 2½cm (1in) thick. Into this area, a layer of top soil, including chopped turves and fibrous roots, is placed about 10cm (4in) deep, and a light dusting of lime is given if the pH reading of the original soil demands it. The bed is turned three or four times during the autumn and early winter period (June–August), to help turves rot down and break up the soil. A layer of well-rotted stable manure is then incorporated and a light dressing of blood and bone given to the bed. After this has all been worked into the bed, provided the soil is nicely moist, it is then trodden down, making it reasonably firm. After lightly raking the surface, all will be ready for planting from the end of September and during October.

Cuttings are taken during the last week in July and the first week in August and this is done in the conventional way from the tips of basal growths. About 5cm (2in) in length when prepared, they are fully immersed in a dish of Parathion or Metasystox while a batch of another cultivar is prepared. The first batch is then planted in a previously prepared nursery bed in the open ground as frosts, if any, are not sufficiently severe to harm plants.

When well-rooted, plants are moved into the growing beds, being placed 45cm (18in) apart in each direction, and are firmed in by treading around the plant. Planting of beds is usually completed by the end of October.

General cultivation such as stopping, side-shooting and lightly hoeing between plants is now carried out in the same fashion as in Britain.

No supplementary feeding is given until the end of January, when a top dressing of rotted stable manure, blood and bone, sulphate of potash, magnesium sulphate and a sprinkling of sulphate of iron is applied and then covered with a 5cm (2in) layer of virgin soil. It is again to be noted that no extra nitrogen is given, which is contrary to the generally accepted practice in England.

Pest and disease control is maintained by fortnightly spraying on a rota basis of Parathion, Metasystox and DDT (now banned in this country), to which is added Benlate for controlling fungus and mildew diseases. An additional dusting of flowers of sulphur is also given to assist in controlling mildew.

Staking is done by providing a short central stake and, as stems develop after stopping, a longer individual stake is given to each of the retained breaks, usually three to a plant. With cultivars that are prone to splitting of the stem immediately under the bud, four breaks are retained and the stems are slit carefully with a penknife when the florets are first visible in the bud. Watering at this time is kept to the minimum, also to help control this splitting.

Protective covering using PVC sheeting is given in early April, approximately one month before the shows in May.

Types of blooms shown are large and medium exhibition, exhibition incurves, reflexes, singles, anemone, spiders, quills and charms, but there are some differences in show regulations.

No supporting rings are allowed and all blooms have to be shown with their own foliage, dummy foliage not being allowed on large exhibition cultivars. Another criticism levelled at us in this country from Tas Jones is that he considers that judges in this country give awards to younger blooms than they would in Tasmania; similarly, and here I would agree, too much emphasis is often given in England to size at the expense of form.

Finally, it would appear that at the present time there is a degree of apathy on the part of the public who do not support shows in the way they should; in this respect we have perfect agreement as, except perhaps for our London national and a few of the larger provincial shows, many of the local societies in Britain suffer the same fate.

Canada

It is rather depressing that each of the countries I have contacted reports the same sad fact that there is difficulty in attracting members of the public to its shows. In Vancouver, this has been partly solved by some of the large enclosed shopping centres offering to pay all expenses if a show is held in the centre. One of the best shows staged in this way is held at Guilford, and it is hoped that this will be extended.

Although there are many chrysanthemum growers in Canada, once more it is distance that is the chief enemy as there are more than 3,000 miles between the west and east areas.

In Victoria, British Columbia, on the western coast, growing conditions are probably as good as any for chrysanthemums in Canada. Winters are usually no more severe than our own and although daytime temperatures soar during the summer months, the nights are cooler because of the effect of the sea which almost surrounds Victoria. Cultivation follows very closely that practised in Britain; rooting cuttings, stopping and timing are all close to our times. Most of the cultivars grown are of the English early-flowering types. Very few lates are grown, as many chrysanthemum growers apparently do not heat their greenhouses.

During the summer months, long dry periods are experienced, and this calls for regular artificial watering—the chief difference between conditions in Victoria as compared to our own.

To illustrate further the strong British influence, all shows are judged according to the judging rules of our own NCS. Classification too is the same as ours and, in fact, when examining the show schedule of the Victoria and District Chrysanthemum Society annual early-flowering show, it could easily be mistaken for the schedule of one of our societies, with one exception which I think we could well adopt. Sections in the schedule gradually school a new grower from the novice stage to the more experienced grade. This is done by having first year, second year and third year novice divisions. For example, a second year novice is a person who has previously exhibited in chrysanthemum shows for not more than one year; an exhibitor in this category can enter all classes in the show except first year novice. Similarly a third year novice will not have entered for more than two years and can show in all sections other than first and second year divisions. This is a slight extension of our own novice and intermediate sections and could certainly be introduced to some effect to encourage new exhibitors at our larger shows, such as the London national, without detracting from the show.

One of the biggest problems for Canadian growers is obtaining the new British introductions. Every plant entering Canada from Britain is first inspected and packed under Ministry of Agriculture inspectors in this country; on arrival in Canada it is quarantined for sixty days under the supervision of the Canadian Department of Agriculture. This is to control disease, in particular the possibility of introducing white rust. The introduction of novelties of most of the British breeders is being greatly facilitated at the present time by Hall's Nurseries, which is collecting, packing and arranging the aircraft collection for its own and other nurseries' novelties. This is reflected in the lists of cultivars shown in 1972 and 1973 where in each year over seventy cultivars, all of British origin, were detailed. For example, in 1972, class 24b (medium reflexed) included 'Barry Wiggins', 'Eve Gray', 'Mayfield', 'Juanita', 'Regalia', 'Early Red Cloak', 'Tourist', 'Leprechaun', 'Impact', and 'Broadway', while in 1973, class 24a (large reflexed) was dominated by 'John Riley', 'Shirley Victoria', 'Grace Riley', 'Golden Standard', 'Parasol', 'Goya', 'Mexico', 'Cecely Starmer', 'Salmon Tracy Waller' and 'Dorothy Gosling'. These could quite easily be taken as lists from our shows in London.

Farther east in Ontario, conditions for chrysanthemum growing are more difficult; being inland, very high temperatures are experienced during the summer months. July and August are particularly hot, with daytime temperatures reaching 32°C (90°F) quite regularly, with only a slight drop at night. Humidity is high and, with little or no rain, artificial watering is the order of the day. In spite of these conditions, the Canadian Chrysanthemum Society, although based in Toronto, has a membership spread right across the country, and during the centennial year celebrations in 1967 a special international chrysanthemum class staged at the annual show attracted entries from Scotland, England and Wales. I look forward to the day when possibly there will regularly be classes of a similar nature in all the major chrysanthemum-growing countries; even now I think this is only prevented by the cost of air transport for blooms.

Europe

Generally, throughout Europe, white chrysanthemums are looked upon as a funeral flower more than anything else. It is difficult to find amateur growers and certainly chrysanthemum societies as we know them do not appear to exist. However, smaller cut-flower and pot chrysanthemums for decorative purposes are now being produced and bought in very large numbers in most European countries.

In Germany there are few amateur growers specializing in chrysanthemums, and certainly no national chrysanthemum society. This is
partly due to the association with death, but commercially, chrysanthemum growing is a very profitable nursery business. The chief
attractions are pots of dwarf-growing chrysanthemums in many
colours other than white. The number of these produced each year
is in excess of 10 millions and a very comprehensive study of commercial chrysanthemum growing has been made in Germany. Cultivation follows the same pattern as in Britain, many nurseries using
the controlled heat and light technique of producing dwarf pot plants
in the same manner as large commercial nurseries do in this country.
'Golden Princess Anne', 'Princess Anne', 'Woking Scarlet' and
the pompons 'Cameo' and 'Denise' are a few examples of cultivars
used.

As well as decorative cultivars grown for cut-flower purposes some
spiders, anemones, cascades and miniature anemones are also grown
for market use.

In Italy again, chrysanthemums are produced extensively on commercial lines, but there is still the thought of death hovering in the
background. During the autumn months of October and November
large numbers of spray chrysanthemums are sold, but a considerable
number of these finish up in cemeteries and churches. Probably in
Italy there has been more of a breakthrough for using chrysanthemums as normal decorative flowers than in most other parts of
Europe but it is rare to find a gardener interested in growing chrysanthemums to perfection in an amateur way.

In Holland it is more or less the same story from the amateur
viewpoint, yet commercially, chrysanthemums are a very large and
important crop grown both in the open and under glass. The Dutch,
expert as they are in all phases of cultivation, have really learnt the
art of commercial chrysanthemum growing from visits made to
Britain; this is one area in which we excel.

Whether or not the British influence in the European Community
will encourage amateur gardeners and amateur growers of chrysanthemums in other parts of Europe on a much larger scale is a matter
for some conjecture. I must, in all honesty, voice the opinion that I
cannot see this happening to any great extent. As far as chrysanthemums are concerned, tradition is likely to die hard, and I do not think
the shadow of the 'funeral flower' will be easily overcome any more
than in this country where there is a similar association with large
white sheath lilies.

New Zealand

Chrysanthemum growing in New Zealand is a different story. As in Britain there is a very keen following and, if anything, the impression gained when browsing through the *Bulletin* of the New Zealand National Chrysanthemum Society is that chrysanthemum shows in New Zealand are more social occasions than they are in Britain. This is probably brought about by the fact that two national shows travel around the country each year, one in the north island and the other in the south, but the major New Zealand championship show alternates between the two islands: one year the north island has the major show with the secondary show in the south island, and the positions are reversed for the following year. The national shows are not held at any fixed venue; instead, they are rotated around the islands, hosted by affiliated chrysanthemum clubs and horticultural societies applying for a national show.

The successful society acts as host, and the national show is then run in conjunction with its own local show. Apart from prize money, entry cards and trophies supplied by the national body, all other arrangements such as halls, vases, staging facilities and entertainment is furnished and arranged by the local society; it is this that goes a long way towards creating the social atmosphere. Each society extends all the hospitality it can to visiting members, many of whom will have travelled long distances. At one particular show, all the visiting national society members found that their hotel or motel rooms had been decorated with bowls of flowers by members of the host society, such is the welcome that is extended to visitors. It is to be admitted that with smaller communities it is possible to exploit the social occasion more, but I am also certain that here in Britain, outside the larger cities such as London or Birmingham, it would not be difficult to adopt a similar system adjusted to our different climate. I could well sum up this aspect of chrysanthemum growing in New Zealand by quoting from the opening speech of the Mayor of Wairnate when the national show was held there:

> Coming together is the beginning
> Keeping together is progress
> Thinking together is unity
> And working together is success.

On the cultural and exhibiting side in New Zealand, the first major difference, obvious to many, is that the season is opposite to ours, main shows being held at the end of April and in early May. These cater almost exclusively for late-flowering cultivars as we know them. Although many British early-flowering cultivars have been introduced into New Zealand, they have not yet made sufficient impact, due to the warm weather conditions, for them to be shown. They are, however, cultivated for garden decoration.

Judging is carried out on a similar pattern to ours, but the classification list varies in some details. Large and medium exhibition cultivars are basically the same as our sections 1 and 2, though some cultivars still considered by us as large may be medium under the New Zealand classification. Section 3, exhibition incurves, does not contain different sections for large and mediums, but when showing, the schedule caters for this by having classes for blooms over and under 15cm (6in) in diameter. The decorative section varies considerably by being spread over three sections: section 4, reflexed decoratives; section 5, intermediate decoratives; and section 6, incurving decoratives. The standards here are governed by the rule when classifying a cultivar; if it is at least 80 per cent reflexed or incurving it is classified accordingly; if it cannot come within either of these categories it is then an intermediate. Some examples will no doubt help to understand this particular system: 'Joy Hughes', 'Shirley Garnet' and 'Symbol' are reflexed decoratives; 'Balcombe Perfection', 'Fair Lady' and 'Harmony' are intermediate; while 'Daily Mirror', 'Diplomat' and 'Mayford Supreme' are incurving.

Section 7 caters for all singles, while sections 8 to 13 look after anemone-centred, pompons, cascades, fantasies and hirsutes. Section 20 covers all early-flowering decorative cultivars and again large and medium are not distinguished but in this section the cultivar is indicated as reflexed, intermediate and incurving to agree with the section 4, 5 and 6 classifications.

The pointing system is still in line with ours, the standard table being form 25, size 25, freshness 25, colour 15, foliage 5 and staging 5. On the question of size, an interesting comment was made in the official New Zealand *Bulletin* of July 1972 when a plea was made to exhibitors to keep the size of decoratives down below six inches as there were still a few a little on the large side which tend to unbalance the class, thus detracting from the decorative effect. Apparently size has not yet been made the god that many exhibitors and judges worship in Britain. Growing conditions are similar to those in Tasmania: special raised beds are constructed about 10cm (4in) above surrounding ground level to allow for adequate drainage. I imagine that this is advised for two reasons; firstly, with the hot dry summers, a considerable amount of artificial watering is necessary; and secondly, when rain does come it is likely to be more of the thunderstorm type when a lot falls in a short while—drainage under such conditions must be good if there is to be no waterlogging. Soil is prepared in mid-September by adding to the surface new topsoil plus well-rotted turf (another reason for raised beds), and a liberal application of animal manure or compost is also given. In mid-October a base fertilizer at a handful to the sq metre (sq yard) is added and pricked into the top of the beds. A light dressing of lime is given only if the pH scale is well below 6·5, so a soil test is needed to decide whether or not lime is applied. Planting is carried out in mid-November, making plants firm but not ramming the soil too much.

The treatment for stopping is very different from our own system. This is no doubt partly due to the fact that late-flowering plants in the open are being dealt with, as opposed to our earlies in the open and lates in pots. Generally the New Zealand grower is advised to cut the plant back by about a third, as this not only encourages branches to develop but also makes them grow more robust and vigorous than if only the extreme tip is pinched. This system of firm cutting back also helps to prevent plants growing too tall, quite a problem with late cultivars growing under the conditions experienced in New Zealand. Large and medium exhibition cultivars are stopped about the middle of December and three breaks are allowed to grow with the usual side-shooting and securing of buds until blooms mature.

Exhibition incurves are allowed to carry six blooms per plant, which is achieved by two stoppings; the first about 7 December, from which three breaks are allowed to grow; and a second stopping about mid-January, when two breaks on each stem are retained giving a total of six. Buds are secured about the end of February. Decoratives are stopped twice, in early December and mid-January, only this time a final total of nine blooms per plant are retained. It will be fairly obvious to growers in this country that form and quality are the prime aims rather than size.

Staking, tying, spraying against pests and diseases and protection of blooms follow the usual accepted pattern.

Supplementary feeding is given in the form of two top dressings, one in mid-January and the second in mid-February, using the following mixture as recommended in the New Zealand Chrysanthemum Society *Bulletin*.

Mid-January
4 parts superphosphate
2 parts bone flour
1 part dried blood
1 part sulphate of potash
½ part sulphate of ammonia

Mid-February
2 parts superphosphate
1 part sulphate of potash
½ part Epsom salts

Both dressings are applied at 50–75g (approx 2–3oz) per sq metre (sq yard).

Further liquid feeds once or twice a week, of diluted manure water alternated with Maxicrop, are given from the time buds are secured until they burst and show colour, when all feeding ceases.

The taking of cuttings is probably the only other phase of culture left to describe. Taken around 10 September, the only real difference here is the recommended rooting medium which is not heard of very often in these days of soil-less compost: four-fifths sharp sand or coarse pumice and one-fifth compost or peat. Cuttings, once rooted in trays or boxes, are transferred to temporary nursery beds of good soil until ready for planting into permanent beds. Most of the deviations from our own methods are due to the fact that the hotter weather conditions demand different treatment in New Zealand.

In concluding this section about other countries, I regret that I am unable to cover all the countries in the world. Japan specializes in some of the more exotic forms of chrysanthemum, while the Canary Islands play an integral part of the commercial cultivation of 'all the year round' chrysanthemums, to quote two further examples, but in common with most of Europe, there is little, if any, amateur influence. This amateur side of chrysanthemum culture, in the main, appears to be the prerogative of the English-speaking races.

16 *Recommended Cultivars*

With the large number of new cultivars introduced each year, any list rapidly becomes out of date; yet no book on chrysanthemum culture would be complete without some guide to cultivars which are expected to be with us for a few years before new ones take their place. Generally, late-flowering cultivars seem to last very much longer; indeed it would be very difficult to replace 'Duke of Kent' or 'Jessie Habgood' in the large exhibition section, yet these were first registered in 1938 and 1948 respectively. In the medium section, 'Cossack' (1943) and 'Connie Mayhew' (1951) have also stood the test of time, though admittedly the latter first appeared on the scene as an exhibition incurve. It is in the realms of the early-flowering cultivars that change is more rapid, yet, although some cultivars may only last a few years, 'Cricket' (1961), 'Crown of Gold' (1963), 'Gladys Sharpe' (1960), 'Keystone' (1963) and 'Tracey Waller' (1963) are still popular though they are all at least ten years old.

My list is drawn from reliable cultivars grown in Britain, but a considerable number of these will give equally good results in America, Australia or New Zealand. However, there may be some cultivars grown in these countries which I have not mentioned. My advice, therefore, to anyone starting to grow, is to first join a national or large society in their own country where they will meet experienced growers who will readily supplement this list if requested.

LATE-FLOWERING CHRYSANTHEMUMS

Large Exhibition

Duke of Kent Large white reflexing bloom, which was raised by that very well-known Australian, T. W. Pockett. Although a very old cultivar it still cannot be beaten; it tends to flower early, so later cuttings are advised. 'Cream Duke' and 'Yellow Duke of Kent': colour sports that are also well worth growing.

Gigantic Very large bloom of a pleasant salmon-bronze colour, generally reflexing; the tips of some florets usually incurve to show the reverse colour. An essential cultivar for any grower in this section.

Harry Gee A lovely shade of pink, large reflexing bloom of good form. Dwarf grower, sometimes difficult to hold for shows as the centre tends to go very quickly. Excellent white and apricot sports.

James Bryant A chestnut-red, often criticized as being too small for the large section, but if good stock is obtained it can still be grown well though its size will never bear comparison to 'Duke of Kent'.

Jessie Habgood Large, broad-shouldered, white reflexing bloom, excellent for exhibition. Foliage of plant usually on the yellow side, even if not over-watered. Florets do not damp very often. Also good primrose-coloured sports of same form.

Keith Luxford Incurving bloom, purple-pink in colour. Needs very early rooting to obtain blooms in time for shows.

Leviathian A very large reddish-bronze reflexing bloom, classified as an 'other' colour under the British classification.

Lilac Prince Large, pale pink bloom with reflexing florets that interlace. Very solid bloom and useful for multi-vase exhibits.

Mark Woolman Large yellow bloom with incurved florets. Can sometimes be difficult to develop from the opening of bud stage if over-fed.

Shirley Primrose Synonymous with 'Patricia Barnett'. Pale yellow incurving bloom, possibly one of the largest Japs in cultivation. Can give a coarse bloom, so it is better if flowered on a natural break second crown after a first stopping in early/mid-March.

Medium Exhibition

Connie Mayhew Large pale yellow bloom which, if not over-restricted, will give true incurved form; a very tall grower.

Cossack Dwarf-growing deep crimson, classical reflexing bloom which will stand feeding. Highly recommended.

Lundy A fairly recent addition to this section. A large, solid, white reflexed bloom.

Surrey White White incurving bloom of good size, with waxlike texture to the florets.

Tropical Lady Deep rose-pink incurving bloom which is likened by some growers to a smaller version of Woking Rose, although a much paler colour.

Exhibition Incurves

LARGE-FLOWERED

Eva Randall Rich bronze colour with firm florets that finish as a perfect ball.

Mavis Shoesmith Attractive pink, strong grower which is fairly easy to grow.

Polar Gem True white incurve with good keeping qualities; should be allowed to carry a larger crop of flowers, about six, to avoid bad-shaped, lumpy blooms.

Shirley Model First-class cultivar of classic form, mauve-purple in colour, it finishes as a perfect ball, but not the easiest cultivar to grow well. Red sport finishes exactly the same as parent, making a wonderful pair.

Welcome News Amber-bronze incurve of good shape. Plant has very compact habit.

Woolman's Perfecta Very solid white bloom of good form, though it can be a little egg-shaped at times. Finishes very well.

Woolman's Royal Rich rosy-purple with silver reverse to florets; good size for exhibition.

MEDIUM-FLOWERED

Brett Williams Wide-petalled yellow bloom of excellent form.

Dorothy Foley Attractive, tight incurved pink bloom with perfect globular form. Upright, neat grower.

Maylen Ivory-white, strong-growing incurve with golden and buff coloured sports.

Minstrel Boy Possibly the best form of all incurves, being a perfect ball. Darker colour underneath, it can sometimes be a little soft when fully mature but is well worth growing. Yellow sport has equally good form and colour possibly more attractive than parent.

Ron Shoesmith Small white bloom, but very compact and having true incurve form.

Vera Woolman Old cultivar, yellow in colour but with really hard florets; slight greenish tinge towards the centre of the bloom.

Waterloo Rich bronze with reddish reverse, rather an unusual colour but a solid neat bloom that does not damp.

Reflexed Decoratives

LARGE-FLOWERED

Bridal Gown Strong, compact plant with classical reflex form. White with a shading of peach colour.

Crimson Lake Large velvet-crimson bloom. An old cultivar introduced in 1954 by Shoesmith, but still makes a good show bloom.

Elizabeth Woolman Beautiful lilac-pink bloom, giving a perfect, nicely overlaid, reflexed bloom. Salmon sport is as good as the parent.

Jim Draycott Large white reflex of good breadth and depth. A recent introduction which should do very well.

Ron James Large yellow broad-shouldered bloom with good depth.

Walker's Jewel Pale pink, perfect reflexing bloom, well-suited to both exhibition and cut-flower.

MEDIUM-FLOWERED

Capri Neat, rich purple bloom with nice form; can flower early, so a late start with rooting cuttings is advised.

Golden Princess Anne Very rich golden-yellow, which is equally good for large specimen plants and small pot culture.

Joy Hughes Carnation pink with slightly spiky florets. Very good medium-sized bloom for exhibition.

Penguin Strong healthy grower of fully reflexing white florets.

Regency An excellent purple medium but requires more plants than usual to be grown to obtain a good matching set of five blooms at the same time.

Shirley Garnet An old stager with rich chestnut-red florets. Still very useful for exhibition and cut-flower purposes.

Stuart Shoesmith Glowing amber-bronze reflex that is reasonably easy to grow.

Intermediate Decoratives

LARGE-FLOWERED

Balcombe Perfection Amber-bronze with red reverse, a well-tried, large incurving bloom. If given two stoppings, the second in mid-July, blooms will be obtained in December and possibly for Christmas. Very good golden and red sports with same characteristics as parent.

Beacon Dwarf grower with bright red and gold incurving florets. An extremely good exhibition cultivar.

Daily Mirror Plum-coloured bloom with silver reverse to florets. Vigorous grower with matching crimson-coloured sport.

Fair Lady Very attractive, pink incurving bloom, but do not over-feed as it is rather prone to damping of florets. Also has an intensive orange colour sport with same formation as parent.

Fred Shoesmith White with cream centre, mostly used for cut-flowers. Should flower for Christmas if given two stoppings.

Golden Gown Rich golden incurved bloom, equally good for exhibition or cut-flowers.

Gold Foil Attractive yellow bloom which is almost a true incurve. Stiff stems, but care must be taken to ensure wood ripens properly as any unripe soft stems will possibly not be sufficiently strong to hold bloom erect.

Olympic Queen Very large pink with silver reverse; a true incurving type of bloom that can be grown to a good size for exhibition.

Purple Glow Lovely purple bloom of recent introduction which is a welcome addition to this section of the classification.

MEDIUM-FLOWERED

Brenda Till Pale yellow bloom having flowers of good form.

New Era Rich pink, hard-petalled bloom which, although on the small side, has excellent form and therefore is highly recommended for show purposes.

Woking Perfection Bright red incurving bloom which can be best described as a smaller version of 'Red Balcombe Perfection', though the colour is a little brighter.

Anenome-centred

LARGE-FLOWERED

Long Island Beauty A good white with yellow cushion centre, several excellent colour sports as well.

Marion Stacey Deep rich rose colour with white cushion. Classified as a purple.

Raymond Mouncey Very good red anemone-centre from the famous Woolman stable.

MEDIUM-FLOWERED

Red Rolinda   Sport from 'Rolinda', but although prefixed by 'Red' is more bronze in appearance and bears bronze colour classification.

Thora   Although first registered in 1916, this pink anemone still gives an extremely good bloom.

Singles

LARGE-FLOWERED

Albert Cooper   Very large yellow, highly recommended for showing.

Broadacre   Dwarf-growing plant with broad white florets and distinctive yellow centre.

Crimson Crown   Bright crimson, as the name implies. Compact upright grower.

Midlander   Rich chestnut-bronze that finishes well. The disk is mostly yellow but has a green centre to it.

Peggy Stevens   Bright yellow, possibly one of the largest singles in cultivation.

Preference   Pale pink florets which shade to white where they join the central disk.

Woolman's Glory   Very good bronze with several rows of florets but most growers prefer the red sport which, although it has the same form and habit as its parent, is a much more attractive colour.

MEDIUM-FLOWERED

Alice Fitton   Rosy purple with very neat foliage.

Chesswood Beauty   Very rich crimson ray florets with a gold central disk. Of perfect form it is one of the most reliable singles.

Edwin Painter   Rich golden-apricot florets which make a solid flower suitable for exhibition or decoration.

Jinx   Very good, pure white flower. Plants will carry a large crop of first-class blooms.

Mason's Bronze   Beautiful bronze bloom, parent of the sport 'Chesswood Beauty'.

Nancy Sherwood   Dwarf-growing plant with attractive lemon-yellow blooms.

American Sprays

Aglow   Bright orange-bronze single.

Artic   Beautiful cream white double flowers.

Christmas Greeting   Lovely deep red double flowers which as the name implies can be flowered for Christmas.

Elegance   White double blooms with pale primrose coloured centre.

Fandango   Very decorative cerise coloured double flowers.

Taffeta   Pink double blooms, also excellent bronze coloured sport.

Tuneful   Delightful bronze single blooms, yellow sport is particularly attractive.

Yellow Hurricane   Bright yellow double flowers supported on stiff stems.

RAYONNANTE, SPIDERY, SPOONS

RAYONNANTES   Unusual blooms with long thin quilled petals flowering from late September to December. Can be grown as disbudded blooms or as sprays. Bronze, pink, white and yellow in colour.

SPIDERY

Cyrillus   Lilac pink in colour with green centres, spiky florets.

Sondra Gail   Unusual red-bronze colour with the typical spider form.

Nightingale   A unique green shaded spider cultivar much liked for floral decoration.

Tokyo   Pure white highly recommended spider bloom.

Tioga   A bright yellow spider with full centred medium tube flowers.

Yellow Knight   Deep yellow, strong stems and is a good grower.

SPOONS

Edmundo   Lilac colour with green centre.

Lamont   Large white spooned single with green centre also very attractive yellow sport.

Magdalena   Delightful golden yellow spoon.

Scintillation   Large flowered pink double blooms.

EARLY FLOWERING CHRYSANTHEMUMS

Incurved Decoratives

LARGE-FLOWERED

Ermine   A perfect white incurved bloom, still much admired, and although first registered in 1955, can still be grown well. Primrose-coloured sport also very good.

Pat Amos   Large white bloom but plants usually grow very tall, making them suitable only for exhibition. Also a pale yellow sport with same habit as parent.

Margaret Riley   A pretty pink dwarf-growing incurve which is much admired. Also white, yellow and bronze sports of which the white is probably most popular.

MEDIUM-FLOWERED

Hilton   Very strong-growing white incurve of good habit and neat foliage.

Iris Riley   Mauve-pink with waxy sheen to florets.

Marjorie Boden   A neat golden-yellow incurve of impeccable form.

Nancy Matthews   Although on the small side, this white incurve is possibly one of the best ever raised for near-perfect globular form.

Skipper   Golden-bronze incurve, with dwarf, upright-growing habit.

Reflexed Decoratives

LARGE-FLOWERED

Alpine Snow   A gleaming white reflex of classical form, with blooms carried on strong erect stems.

Brian Russon   Very large, broad-shouldered bloom, excellent for exhibition as very little dressing required.

Bruera   An outstanding white reflex, broad-shouldered and deep florets which fold back almost to the stem. Also exceptionally good primrose sport with same form as parent.

Cecely Starmer   Rose-pink, hard-petalled reflex that resists damping; medium height and compact-growing plant.

Grace Riley   A large bronze bloom with very good form. Dwarf-growing but best restricted to two blooms per plant for exhibition. Scarlet-red sport of same form retains its colour very well.

Smart Fella Dwarf-growing plant with blooms of nice yellow colour and good size. Very resistant to damping of florets.

Tracy Waller Carnation-pink bloom with slightly whorled florets. Rather a thin, tall grower, but exceptionally good for exhibition, though protection is necessary to avoid loss of colour. 'Cherry', 'Salmon' and 'Bronze' sports of which the salmon is the largest and consequently most popular with most exhibitors.

MEDIUM-FLOWERED

Alice Jones Short sturdy grower with light bronze blooms which are large for a medium.

Bellair Purple bloom which is excellent for garden decoration but may be considered by many growers to be too small for exhibition.

Broadway Lovely purple-red bloom with contrasting silver reverse.

Early Red Cloak Bright scarlet blooms, very reliable grower equally good for exhibition or decoration.

Eve Gray Perfect medium-pink reflex for exhibition. Quite hardy when grown outside. Bronze sport is as attractive as parent.

Gipsy Large scarlet reflexing bloom of fine form. Extremely vivid colour which does not fade.

Karen Rowe Pale pink with full centre and perfect form. Vigorous grower but grows a little on the tall side.

Leprechaun Cerise pink of good reflexing form similar to that of 'Eve Gray'.

Mexico This large bloom, recently re-classified in the medium section, is of an unusual shade of red which will undoubtedly have a new lease of life as a medium.

Value Good light bronze of classical reflex form, but is only recommended for exhibition. Yellow sport with same qualities as parent.

Woolley Dandy Brilliant flame-red with gold centre, small shiny foliage on reasonably dwarf-growing plant.

Intermediate Decoratives

LARGE-FLOWERED

Christine Hall Delicate pale pink of large size and perfect incurving intermediate form. White sport is ideal subject for bag protection.

Crown of Gold Rich golden-yellow with hard petals, making a superb exhibition bloom.

Ethel Edmonds A loosely incurving intermediate, oyster-cream in colour. The golden sport is probably more vigorous than the parent.

Flo Cooper Dwarf yellow with bloom similar in appearance to 'Gladys Sharpe'. Highly recommended.

Gladys Sharpe Rich yellow of good size and quality. Vigorous and easy to grow and very reliable for exhibition.

Keystone Purple with silver reverse of classical incurving form. Beautiful show cultivar with red and bronze sports which both have the contrasting reverse colour.

Shirley Victoria Very large incurving chestnut-amber bloom of good size. Strong, healthy, compact plant with strong stems.

Yes Sir Solid white intermediate of good size. One of the best large intermediates introduced in recent years.

MEDIUM-FLOWERED

Alistair Doig An unusual bronze-coloured intermediate which is almost a true incurve. Recommended as something just a little different.

Bill Else Bright yellow, similar in form to the famous 'Cricket'.

Bonigold Another excellent yellow, with blooms almost incurved, which stands up to bad weather extremely well even if unprotected.

Cricket One of the better-known mediums which has almost become a legend. Yellow and primrose sports make an almost perfect trio that all exhibitors should grow. Also very good for garden decoration.

Dairy Cream Pale yellow bloom, aptly named; finished in the centre almost tight enough to be classified as an incurve.

Lyngford Rich rosy-purple with silver reverse, classified as pink. Very suitable exhibition cultivar for multi-vase work to give good range of colour to an exhibit.

Pendower Glistening white with crisp hard petals, similar in appearance to 'Cricket'.

Sombrero Tightly incurving, rich golden-yellow, which will grow well covered or unprotected for both exhibitor and general garden use.

Tibshelf Gem Very weatherproof, hard-petalled deep yellow cultivar.

Pompons

Andy Pandy   Very free-flowering yellow.
Bright Eye   Attractive golden-yellow with red eye.
Cameo   One of the best dwarf-growing whites.
Denise   Reliable dwarf-growing yellow.
Fairie   Pink, with many coloured sports of same form and habit.
   Bronze and salmon sports are to be recommended for variation
   of colour.

Sprays

There are many excellent sprays listed in nurserymen's catalogues, all
of which can be recommended. Those bearing the name 'Hoek', e.g.
'Gerrie Hoek' and 'Lilian Hoek', and others prefixed by the name
'Pennine', e.g. 'Pennine Yellow', are all highly recommended.

Koreans

Numerous cultivars are again listed, all excellent for border decoration. Personal preference as to colour and form will decide which to
choose.

Appendix A

Conversion Tables

LENGTH

centimetres	feet/inches	feet/inches	centimetres
1	approx 0·4″	1″	approx 2·5
5	2″	3″	7·5
10	4″	6″	15
15	6″	9″	22·5
20	8″	1′ 0″	30·5
25	10″	1′ 6″	45·5
50	1′ 8″	2′ 0″	61
75	2′ 6″	2′ 6″	75
100 (1 metre)	3′ 3″	3′ 0″	91·5

WEIGHT

grammes	ounces	ounces	grammes
50	approx 1¾	1	approx 28
100	3½	2	56
125	4¼	5	142
250	8¾	8 (½lb)	227
500	1lb 1½	12	340
1,000 (1 kilo)	2lb 3	16 (1lb)	453

LIQUID

litres	pints/gallons	gallons	litres
1	approx 1¾ pints	⅛ (1 pint)	0·57
2	3½	¼ (2 pints)	1·15
3	5¼	½ (4 pints)	2·3
4	7	¾ (6 pints)	3·4
5	1·1 gallons	1	4·5
6	1·3	2	9·1
7	1·5	3	13·6
8	1·8	4	18·2
9	2·0	5	22·7
10	2·2	6	27·3

TEMPERATURES

To convert Centigrade to Fahrenheit, multiply by 9, divide by 5 and add 32. To convert Fahrenheit to Centigrade, subtract 32, multiply by 5, and divide by 9.

Fahrenheit	Centigrade	Fahrenheit	Centigrade
212 (boiling)	100	41	5
104	40	32 (freezing)	0
86	30	28	− 2
77	25	23	− 5
68	20	18	− 8
59	15	5	−15
50	10	0	−18

USA MEASURES AND EQUIVALENTS

Definitions for the international pound and yard adopted in 1959 bring USA weights and measures into correspondence with those of the UK, with the exception of the USA measurements of capacity which include both dry and liquid pints and quarts, the dry derived from the bushel (64 dry pints = 1 bushel) and the liquid from the gallon (8 liquid pints = 1 US gallon).

The short ton of 2,000lb and the short hundredweight of 100lb are used more commonly in the USA than in the UK.

USA dry measure equivalents
         1 pint — 0·9689   UK pt — 0·5506 litres
         1 bushel — 0·9689   UK bu — 35·238 litres

USA liquid measure equivalent
         1 fluid oz   — 1·0408 UK fl oz — 0·0296 litres
         1 pint (16 fl oz) — 0·8327 UK pt   — 0·4732 litres
         1 gallon   — 0·8327 UK gall — 3·7853 litres

Appendix B

Insecticides, Fungicides and Soil Sterilizers

INSECTICIDES

Abol X   Systemic insecticide for controlling aphids. Contains BHC and Menazon.

Azobenzine   Fumigant for use against red spider.

BHC   (Benzene Hexachloride) Controls aphids, capsids, leafminers and thrips.

Derris   Non-poisonous spray for control of aphids and thrips.

Diazinon   Mainly used by commercial growers, an organo-phosphorus insecticide which controls most pests.

Fentro   Containing Fentrothion, this is a liquid spray for controlling capsids and caterpillars. An alternative to DDT, which is now withdrawn by government order.

Lindane   A BHC compound which will control aphids, leafminer, thrips, capsids and most pests.

Malathion   Organo-phosphorus compound which once diluted is comparatively safe to use, though rubber gloves are advised. Controls aphids, thrips and whitefly.

Menazon   Insecticide similar in effect to BHC, though it is said to be partially systemic.

Metasystox   Contact systemic insecticide which kills all sap-sucking insects by being absorbed into a plant's sap stream, either through the foliage or by watering through the root system.

Metaldehyde   Controls slugs; usually applied as a bait but can also be used as a spray.

Nicotine   A highly poisonous but old remedy for controlling most pests, which can be applied either as a spray or smoke fumigant; but as it relies on fumes, it is not effective below 10°C (50°F). Must not be inhaled.

Parathion   Highly poisonous and usually only available to commercial growers; while effective against all sap-sucking insects it is used extensively against eelworm. Protection including rubber gloves and mask must be taken when using Parathion.

Pirimor   Very good control of aphids and most pests. Proprietary name containing Pirimcarb as the active ingredient.

Pyrethrum   Non-poisonous spray or dust for control of aphids, thrips, capsids and froghoppers.

Rapid   Another trade name for effective insecticide containing Pirimcarb.

FUNGICIDES

Benlate   Having systemic action, it is very effective against powdery mildew.

Captan   Controls botrytis and ray blight.

Cheshunt compound   Used to prevent damping off of cuttings. Will not cure those already affected.

Combinex   Effective against fungus diseases such as rust.

Karathane   Available as a dust, wettable powder or smoke, it is usual to control mildew.

Zineb   Excellent fungicide for controlling rust and petal blight.

SOIL STERILIZERS

Basamid   Containing Dazomet, used for control of disease in the soil. Especially effective against verticillium wilt.

Formaldehyde   For sterilization of soil in greenhouse beds.

Jeyes fluid   Very useful to help control spread of disease. Used to water-in stools after lifting, for cleansing greenhouses and watering on soil as digging proceeds.

Appendix C

Chrysanthemum Nurseries

BRITAIN

Elm House Nurseries Ltd, Walpole St Peter, Wisbech, Cambs, Pe14 7PJ

L. Hall, Broad Way Nurseries, High Heath, Pelsall, Walsall, WS4 1AW

C. E. Jefferies, Kelston View Nurseries, Lower Hanham Road, Hanham, Bristol, BS15 2HH.

J. & T. Johnson, The Nurseries, Tibshelf, Derby, DE5 5PD

Riley's, Alfreton Nurseries, Woolley Moor, Derby, DE5 6FF

Harold Walker, Oakfield Nurseries, Huntington, Chester, CH3 6EA

G. Wilson, Three Trees Nursery, Prayle Grove, Cricklewood, NW2 1BB

H. Woolman Ltd, Dorridge, Solihull, West Midlands, B93 8QB

Alan Wren, Beechview Nursery, Avey Lane, Waltham Abbey, Essex

AMERICA

Flower Land, 816 English Street, Racine, Wis 53402

House of Bonsai, William N. Valavanis, 412 Pinnacle Rd, Rochester, NY 14623

King's Chrysanthemums, 3723 E. Castro Valley Blvd, Castro Valley, California 94546

Sunnyslope Gardens, 8638 Huntingdon Dr, San Gabriel, California 91775

Thon's Garden Mums, Dept C, 4815 Oak St, Crystal Lake, Illinois 60014

GERMANY

Ludwig Kientzler, 655 Bad Kreuznach

NEW ZEALAND

Leo Clark, PO Box 12046, Beckenham, Christchurch, New Zealand

Appendix D

BRITAIN

National Chrysanthemum Society Secretary: S. G. Gosling, 65 St Margarets Avenue, Whetstone, London N20

AMERICA

National Chrysanthemum Society of USA Secretary: Mrs Warren A. Christoffers, 394 Central Avenue, Mountainside, New Jersey, 07092. Editor of *Bulletin*: John C. Bayles, 406 Lenox Place, South Orange, NJ 07079. Chairman Handbook Committee: Walter S. Greene, 14008 Glenn Mill Rd, Rockville, Md 20650. Mrs Anne Richardson, 856 SW 174th St, Seattle, Wash 98166

AUSTRALIA

West Australian Chrysanthemum Society Secretary: Mrs M. O. Wright, 70 Star St, Carlisle 6101, Western Australia

Chrysanthemum Study Club of Australia Secretary: Keith Dela-force, 16 Highland Avenue, Bankstown, NSW

Chrysanthemum Section, Hobart Horticultural Society Secretary: Tas Jones, 5 Pickard Street, Lenah Valley, Hobart 7008, Tas-mania

Chrysanthemum Section, Royal Horticultural Society Secretary: H. Harrison, 303 Auburn Rd, Auburn, Victoria

South Australian Floracultural Society Secretary: A. Simcock, 93 Morphet Rd, Morphetville, South Australia

Wodanga & District Horticultural Society Secretary: A. Wilson, 590 Mitchell St, Albury, NSW

K. W. May, 2 Craigie Crescent, Manning 6152, Western Australia

A. Paice, 106 Lansdowne Rd, South Perth

CANADA

New Westminster & District Chrysanthemum Society   Secretary: Mrs E. Skog, 824 Burnaby St, New Westminster, BC

Peace Portal Amateur Chrysanthemum Society   Secretary: John Reuss, 14627 Marine Drive, Whiterock, BC

Point Grey Amateur Chrysanthemum Association   Secretary: J. Gordon Stanton, 1770 W 12th Apt 103 Vancouver, BC

University Chrysanthemum Association   Secretary: W. J. Nelson, 7611 French St, Vancouver, BC

Vancouver Chrysanthemum Club   Secretary: R. Horstead, 2816 E 45th Vancouver, BC

Victoria & District Chrysanthemum Society   President: Mrs Shirley McMinn, 3557 Quadra St, Victoria, BC

Gordon Bentham, 3272 Wicklow Street, Victoria, BC

Mrs J. Dickson, 24 Edenville Drive, West Hill, Ontario

NEW ZEALAND

New Zealand National Chrysanthemum Society   Secretary: K. H. H. Kitney, 96 Glasgow St, Wanganui

Glossary

axil   the angle between the upper side of a leaf or stem and the supporting stem or branch.

basal growths   young growths which sprout from root of plant away from main stem, used for cuttings when propagating

bicolour   a bloom whose petals have two colours, whether on the face (obverse) or reverse

bonsai   the growing of a chrysanthemum in miniature tree form

boxing   act of digging up chrysanthemums at the end of season from open ground and putting in boxes for winter storage

branch   a stem with multiple sprays attached

break   lateral growth obtained from natural break or stopping

break bud   bud which forms naturally on the young main stem, below this bud the plant breaks into fresh branches

chlorosis   yellowing of leaves due to iron deficiency, corrected by the application of sequestrene iron

cultivar   internationally agreed term to describe a plant variant raised as a seedling or sport, better known to most growers under the old inaccurate term 'variety'

cutting   unrooted leafy growth taken from old root or stem

daisy-eyed   a double chrysanthemum in which the outer ray florets fail to obscure the central disk florets

disbudding   removal of unnecessary side-growths and buds other than the main bud to obtain large individual blooms

disk   central portion of the bloom, apparent in single blooms, semi-doubles, anemones and similar blooms other than doubles

disk florets   florets in centre of bloom, not normally seen in a double bloom but forming the central pin cushion in single blooms, either yellow or green in colour

division   splitting up old roots of plants and using younger portions to replant in borders

first crown bud   first bud that appears at the end of a lateral growth

form   approved shape of bloom specified for a particular type of cultivar

habit   general growing nature and appearance of a plant: type of foliage, stem and branching conditions

lateral growth   see break

mutation   change in growth of plant, a sport

mulching   covering ground with organic matter to assist in the retention of moisture

natural break   if plant is left to grow naturally a bud eventually appears on the main stem before the plant branches out: this is known as the break bud

running-on   act of rubbing out first crown bud and allowing one shoot to develop a flower on a second crown bud

ray florets   the long florets which radiate from the centre of a bloom, often referred to as petals

securing the bud   act of removing all side-shoots and buds to leave the main bud to develop into a flower

second crown bud   if the lateral growth is stopped again, further side-shoots develop until these in turn produce a bud known as the second crown bud

sport   a shoot producing a flower different in colour or character from parent plant

spray   final flowering growth consisting of one stem

stool   root of an old plant with portion of old stem attached

stopping   removal of tip of a growth either main stem or side growth to encourage breaks to grow

sucker   rooted shoot springing from old root

terminal bud   bud which develops surrounded by other flower buds, indicating the end of vegetative growth

vernalization   period of rest in cool temperatures after flowering has finished

Bibliography

PUBLISHED BY THE NATIONAL CHRYSANTHEMUM SOCIETY
(GREAT BRITAIN)

Booklet for Newcomers
Chrysanthemum Manual
Exhibiting and Judging
Lates for Learners by E. Morley Jones
List of Judges and *Code of Rules for Judging*
National Register of Cultivars, listed up to 1964
National Register of Cultivars, supplementary edition 1964–1972
Nutrition, by B. Machin
Pests and Diseases of the Chrysanthemum by E. Morley Jones
Progressive Thinking towards Quality Chrysanthemums by Harry
   Randall
Soil and Chrysanthemums by E. Morley Jones

PUBLISHED BY THE NATIONAL CHRYSANTHEMUM SOCIETY INC (USA)

Advanced Growers' Handbook No 5
Beginners' Handbook No 2
Breeders' Handbook No 4
Chrysanthemum Classification Register
Show and Judges' Handbook No 6

OTHER PUBLICATIONS

Chrysanthemem, by Albert Vogelmann (Technische Unwersität,
München, Germany)
Chrysanthemums in New Zealand (National Chrysanthemum Society
   of New Zealand)
Chrysanthemum Book, by Roderick Cummings (D. Van Nostrand
   Co, Princetown, NJ, USA)

Chrysanthemums (manual of culture), edited by Robert W. Langham (New York State Extension Service Chrysanthemum School)

Pocket Encyclopedia of Chrysanthemums in Colour, by Stanley Gosling (Blandford Press Ltd, London)

Wisley Handbook No 11 (*Chrysanthemums*), by James F. Smith (Royal Horticultural Society)

General Index

General Index

Abol X, 183
Acidity of soil, 33
Alkalinity of soil, 33
America, 13–14, 51, 155–9, 170, 185
American National Chrysanthemum Society Inc., 15–16, 155
American sprays, 20–3; stopping, 71; recommended cultivars, 176 *see also* Spray cultivars
Ammonium sulphate, 45, 46
Anemone-centred cultivars, 23, 27; stopping, 65, 69, 74; recommended, 174–5
Aphids, 116–18
Artificial fertilizers, 44–6
Ash base, for growing on, 55–6
Australia, 14, 17, 51, 159–62, 170; Societies in, 187
Axil, 189
Azobenzine, 183

Bagging, 84–6
Basal growths, 52, 102, 189
Basamid, 125, 184
Base fertilizer, 46
Benlate, 89, 184
Benomyl, 89
Bentley's fertilizer, 99, 105
Bernet, Captain, 12
BHC, 88, 117, 118, 119, 120, 123, 183
Bicolour, 189
Birds, protection against, 78, 80, 123

Blancard, Pierre Louis, 12
Blooms, protection of, by bags and covers, 84–6; treatment of for exhibition, 130–7
B9 (height retardent), 86–7
Bone flour, 47
Bonemeal, 43
Bonsai, 13–14, 111–13, 189
Borax, 47
Border chrysanthemums, 24–5
Botanical Magazine, 12
Botrytis, 127
Boxing, 90–1, 189
Break bud, 57, 189
Breaks, 106, 189
Breeding from seed, 149–54
Bregnius, 12
Bud, initiation of, 29–30; break, 57, 189; securing, 58–62, 190; first, second crown, 58, 189, 190; terminal, 190

Calcium, 41
Canada, 162–4; Societies in, 188
Canary Islands, 169
Capsids, 118–19
Captan, 127, 128, 184
Cascades, 24, 107–8
Caterpillars, 119
Charms, 23–4, 49, 105–7
Chemicals in disease control, 115
Cheshunt compound, 126, 184
China, 11
Chlorosis, 189
Chusan daisy, 12

Index of Cultivars

Index of Cultivars